He Is the Christ

Aaron Dolan

Eric Schroeder

NORTHWESTERN PUBLISHING HOUSE
Milwaukee, Wisconsin

Northwestern Publishing House
N16W23379 Stone Ridge Dr., Waukesha, WI 53188
www.nph.net

Published 2025
Printed in the United States of America
ISBN 978-0-8100-3231-6
ISBN 978-0-8100-3232-3 (e-book)

24 25 26 27 28 29 30 31 32 33 10 9 8 7 6 5 4 3 2 1

Contents

God Keeps His Promises
Matthew 1:1 1

Jesus Fulfills Prophecy
Matthew 1:22-23 2

Joy to the World
Matthew 2:10 4

A Sad Reality
Matthew 2:16 5

The Well-Pleased Parent
Matthew 3:17 7

Satisfied by the Word
Matthew 4:4 9

Disciples Keep Learning
Matthew 5:1-2 11

Filled With Righteousness
Matthew 5:6 13

Rejoice in Our Reward
Matthew 5:11-12 14

Fulfillment of the Law
Matthew 5:17 16

But I Tell You . . .
Matthew 5:21-22 17

Is Jesus Serious?
Matthew 5:29-30 19

Yes or No
Matthew 5:37. 20

For Me, for Them, or for God?
Matthew 5:42. 22

Be Perfect
Matthew 5:48. 23

How to Pray
Matthew 6:9 25

Safe Deposit
Matthew 6:20-21 26

First on the List
Matthew 6:33. 28

Look in the Mirror
Matthew 7:5 29

Good Gifts, Good Giver
Matthew 7:11 31

Don't Follow the Crowd
Matthew 7:13. 33

Scary Words
Matthew 7:21. 35

When Hearing Isn't Enough
Matthew 7:24. 36

Just Say the Word
Matthew 8:8 38

The Doctor for Sinners
Matthew 9:13. 40

Ask for Workers
Matthew 9:38. 42

It's Free!
Matthew 10:8 43

Healthy Fear
Matthew 10:28 45

Don't Be Afraid
Matthew 10:30-31 47

How to Love Best
Matthew 10:37 49

Come to Jesus for Rest
Matthew 11:28 51

Should We Tell or Not?
Matthew 12:16 53

The Sign of Jonah
Matthew 12:40 55

A Huge Harvest
Matthew 13:8 57

Leave It to God
Matthew 13:28-29 58

All-In Investment
Matthew 13:44 60

Jesus Caught Him
Matthew 14:31 62

Unclean on the Inside
Matthew 15:19 63

Great Faith
Matthew 15:28 65

Who Is Jesus?
Matthew 16:16 67

Listen to Him
Matthew 17:5 69

A Tax-Free Life
Matthew 17:25-26 71

God's Will and Ours
Matthew 18:14 73

To*, Not *About
Matthew 18:15 75

Forgive From the Heart
Matthew 18:35 76

Back to the Beginning
Matthew 19:4-6 78

A Generous Master
Matthew 20:15 80

A Holy Week of Fulfillment
Matthew 21:4 81

Doubtless Faith
Matthew 21:21-22 83

You Are Chosen
Matthew 22:14 85

Greatness in Service
Matthew 23:11 86

Jesus Longs to Gather
Matthew 23:37 88

Stand Firm to the End
Matthew 24:13,35 90

Be Ready
Matthew 24:44 92

Well Done
Matthew 25:21 93

The Righteous Answer
Matthew 25:37 95

The Perfect Meal
Matthew 26:26-28 97

As God Wills
Matthew 26:39 99

Fulfilled This Way
Matthew 26:53-54 100

No Defense
Matthew 27:14 102

See What He Suffered!
Matthew 27:28-29 104

Forsaken
Matthew 27:46 105

The Curtain Is Torn
Matthew 27:51 107

The Greatest Escape
Matthew 27:65-66 109

Don't Be Surprised
Matthew 28:6. 110

The Right Tools
Matthew 28:19-20 112

Get Ready for Jesus
Mark 1:2,4 114

Attended by Angels
Mark 1:13 116

The Call to Ministry
Mark 1:17-18 118

Jesus Versus the Demon
Mark 1:23-26 120

Go See Jesus, Then Go Serve
Mark 1:30-33 121

A Break for Prayer
Mark 1:35. 123

Jesus Knows Better
Mark 1:43-45 125

Jesus Gives More Than You Ask For
Mark 2:5,10-11 126

Jesus Has the Authority to Forgive Your Sins
Mark 2:10-12 128

It's for You
Mark 2:27-28. 129

Demons Answer the Question
Mark 3:11 131

The "Experts" Answer the Question
Mark 3:21-22 132

Jesus' Family
Mark 3:34-35. 134

His Word Has Power
Mark 4:27 136

Power and Care
Mark 4:38-40. 137

We Should Fear and Love Jesus
Mark 5:6-7,10 139

Jesus Gives Your Life Purpose
Mark 5:18-19 140

Jesus Has Time for You
Mark 5:33-36. 142

Jesus Turns Death Into Sleep
Mark 5:39,41-42 144

How Well Do You Know Jesus?
Mark 6:3 145

Jesus Was Rejected Too
Mark 6:5-6 147

Trust Jesus' Commands
Mark 6:7-8 148

Does God Love Me?
Mark 6:22-24. 150

Jesus Has Compassion
Mark 6:34 152

Jesus Provides for Soul and Body
Mark 6:34,41-42 153

Jesus Gives Courage
Mark 6:45-48,50 155

He Will Heal You
Mark 7:34-35. 156

Jesus Uses People to Provide
Mark 8:6-9 158

Seek First His Kingdom
Mark 8:14-17 160

Jesus Knows Why
Mark 8:23-25. 162

The Job Description
Mark 8:31-33 163

Say No to Yourself
Mark 8:34 165

Jesus Is Serious About Sin
Mark 9:42-43. 166

One Thing You Lack
Mark 10:21-22 168

More Evidence of Jesus' Love
Mark 10:21 169

How to Be Great
Mark 10:43-45 171

Triumphant and Willing
Mark 11:9-10 172

He Sent His Son
Mark 12:6-8 174

Both God and Government
Mark 12:17 175

The God of the Living
Mark 12:24,26-27 177

The Greatest Commandments
Mark 12:33-34 178

David's Son and David's Lord
Mark 12:35,37 180

The Widow's Offering
Mark 12:43 182

She Did What She Could
Mark 14:6,8. 183

The Only Answer That Matters
Mark 14:61-64 185

The Power of Sin
Mark 14:71-72 186

Focus on the Cross
Mark 15:24 188

Jesus Is the Son of God
Mark 15:39 190

He Has Risen!
Mark 16:6. 191

Seated at the Right Hand of God
Mark 16:19 193

Introduction

The People's Bible Devotions series encompasses all the books of the Bible, taking readers into devotional thoughts from Genesis through Revelation. The authors did not write a meditation on every chapter and verse in the Bible, and yet as you read through the series, you will be walking devotionally through the major sections and themes of every book in God's Holy Library.

The book you are holding presents the powerful words of God for your spiritual reflection and growth. Have a Bible or Bible app handy, because each devotion will provide a suggested reading from the Bible as context and then focus your meditation on a specific thought from our Lord in that reading. Where you notice verses and chapters not included in these devotions, accept this encouragement to read these sections of Scripture on your own, since they were inspired by the Holy Spirit and are desirable for growth, guidance, and strength.

Except for one volume, each book of this series is written by a team of authors connected to each other in some way, often as family members. Every author comes to the task with deep training in the Scriptures and rich experience in the public ministry.

This volume covers two gospels, Matthew and Mark. Though both Bible books tell of the life and ministry of Jesus, the Holy Spirit had specific audiences in mind as he guided the authors. Written to a Jewish audience, the book of Matthew points to more than 60 Old Testament prophecies, showing how Jesus' miracles testify that he is the Messiah foretold by all the prophets. Mark's gospel is addressed especially to gentile Romans and focuses attention on Jesus' mighty acts—works that prove he is the Son of God. The devotions in this volume all underscore the fact that the Holy Spirit also had us in mind as he guided the apostles, using their words to teach us what it means that Jesus is the Son of God, our Savior.

Treasure the Bible-based, Christ-centered messages you find here, inspirational for you and countless more in any place or time.

Editor

The authors of this book are Pastors Aaron Dolan and Eric Schroeder. Their friendship began as classmates at Fox Valley Lutheran High School, where they had classes together, played on the football and basketball teams together, and finished first and second in their class. Both credit the pastoral faculty members at FVL, especially their Latin and Church History teacher (Aaron's dad), for influencing their decisions to become pastors. Later, they even served in the same congregation, First Evangelical Lutheran Church, in Racine, Wisconsin. Eric was assigned there as a vicar, and later, Aaron was assigned there as a pastor.

In addition to his service at First Lutheran in Racine, Pastor Dolan has served at Luther Preparatory School, Watertown, Wisconsin; Fox Valley Lutheran High School, Appleton, Wisconsin; and Martin Luther College, New Ulm, Minnesota.

Pastor Schroeder has served at Bloomington Living Hope Lutheran Church, Bloomington and Shakopee, Minnesota; and St. John Lutheran Church, Wauwatosa, Wisconsin.

God Keeps His Promises

Bible Reading: Matthew 1:1-16

This is the genealogy of Jesus the Messiah the son of David, the son of Abraham. (Matthew 1:1)

What is the oldest promise you have kept? For some people, it may be marriage vows. For those raised in the church, it could be confirmation vows. Either way, such promises are intended to last for the rest of a lifetime. Wouldn't it be interesting to view a record of all the promises we've ever made—both the ones we have kept and the ones we have broken?

We probably don't think of genealogies as the most interesting parts of the Bible; after all, they are only lists of names, right? As Matthew began to pen his inspired account of the life and work of Jesus Christ, he started with a genealogy—a record of the promise to Abraham passed down through the generations until it was fulfilled when Jesus was born. God had said that the Savior of the world would come through Abraham and his children, and Matthew traced the bloodline through more than two thousand years of history. In reality, the promise went back much further, long before the time of Abraham, way back to the time sin first entered our world and all of humanity suddenly needed a Savior.

God made a promise for us all; Jesus the Messiah is the fulfillment of that ancient promise. As we read on in Matthew's account, we'll see how Jesus fulfilled every prophecy about the Savior in his life, his work, his suffering and death, and his magnificent resurrection. He is indeed the Messiah—the Anointed One, the perfect Prophet, Priest, and King that sinners need in a Savior.

Some names on this long list may bring back memories of Bible stories we learned as children; others may sound familiar from sermons we have heard. Either way, we realize that if the promise depended on any of these people, it surely would have failed along the way. Instead, we find great comfort in the fact that God was determined to fulfill this promise despite the unfaithfulness of sinful men and women throughout the ages. Despite the wandering of flawed humans, God's promise stayed on track. If we are ever tempted to doubt God and his faithfulness, we need only consider how God kept this ancient promise when he sent his own Son to deliver us. God kept this promise—and he keeps every promise!

Prayer: Father, thank you for reminding me of your faithfulness today. Increase my trust in your promises whenever I consider how you kept your word to send me a Savior. Amen.

E.D.S.

For further reading, see The People's Bible commentary on Matthew, pages 8-17.

Jesus Fulfills Prophecy

Bible Reading: Matthew 1:18-25

All this took place to fulfill what the Lord had said through the prophet: [23] "The virgin will conceive and give birth to a son, and they will call him Immanuel" (which means "God with us"). (Matthew 1:22-23)

"I told you so." Often when those words are spoken, it is in a spirit of pride. Deep down we probably all struggle with the desire to be right, even if—or especially if—it means someone else is wrong. Maybe we guessed correctly about what was going to happen. Perhaps we knew some trivial fact that family members refused to believe until we handed them the fact-checked proof or an eyewitness confirmed what we claimed to be true. Right or wrong, a part of us loves to say, "I told you so."

A recurring theme in Matthew's gospel account is how God "told us so" in the way he predicted who the Savior would be and how the world would be able to identify him when he entered humanity as one of us. All throughout the historical record of the Old Testament, God spoke through his prophets, sharing hundreds of details outlining the Messiah's life and work, including where he would be born, where he would call home, and how he would die. However, God didn't work through prophecy all those years just so he could be right. He fulfilled prophecy so that we could be righteous in his sight forever.

Believers in Old Testament times were saved the same way we are today: by believing the gospel message. Just as we believe that Jesus fulfilled even the most unlikely (humanly speaking) prophetic signs, so our ancestors in the faith believed that the Savior would fulfill every prophecy—all to rescue us from the guilt and punishment that sin requires. God used Isaiah to foretell the virgin birth seven hundred years before it happened, and God used Matthew to assure his readers that the long-awaited Immanuel had come in the flesh—God with us, as one of us—but with a divine holiness that cannot be found in any of us.

Long ago, God "told us so." Now that Immanuel has come, God tells us again. He wants us to know him through his Son. He longs for us to believe what was foretold and now has been fulfilled. How blessed we are to see Jesus as the promised Messiah whose conception is only the beginning of all he would fulfill for us.

Prayer: Holy Spirit, thank you for working through the prophets to give us the signs identifying our Savior and for inspiring Matthew to note their fulfillment in Christ. As we read on, use each sign to strengthen our trust in Jesus. Amen.

E.D.S.

For further reading, see The People's Bible commentary on Matthew, pages 19-23.

Joy to the World

Bible Reading: Matthew 2:1-12

When they saw the star, they were overjoyed. (Matthew 2:10)

Perhaps we can all think of a time when an experience did not live up to our expectations. It might have been a movie that received rave reviews but was so boring it almost put us to sleep. Perhaps it was the new technology that was supposed to be life-changing but came with so many glitches it was almost unusable. Or maybe we waited so long to see a musical artist in person, but the live performance was so disappointing that we wished we could have our ticket money back.

Now think of the Magi. We can't say for sure where their trip started, but it was likely hundreds of miles from their destination. We can only imagine the time, effort, and expense that they invested to follow a star, all in hope of seeing a newborn king. They first checked the palace in Jerusalem (a reasonable move if one were looking for royalty) but were then sent to a small town a few short miles away. Finally, the star they were chasing came to a rest.

What did they find? Was the newborn King everything they were expecting? It's hard to know for certain, but probably not. He was just an average-looking infant. The surroundings were humble; his parents appeared closer to the bottom class of society than the top. We may wonder if there was a moment of confusion or hesitation, or even disappointment, after traveling all that way—for this?

As Matthew describes their meeting, however, he doesn't mention any hesitation—only joy, praise, and worship expressed with their posture and possessions. Isn't it the same in our lives? Perhaps to an untrained eye Jesus seems so human. Actually, that's why we worship him as we do! God's own Son entered flesh just like ours, with all its human frailty, vulnerability, and mortality. The immortal God became killable so that he could be our perfect substitute and bring divine righteousness into our world. He set aside the glory of heaven to humble himself and become our Servant-King, willing even to give his life in our place. He came all the way from heaven to live and die for us!

Maybe Jesus' presence in our lives doesn't look all that impressive. Perhaps it isn't always what we expect. But one day all who trust in him will see him in the glory he once set aside—and God promises that we won't be disappointed. Until then, thinking about our Savior fills us with joy and inspires our worship because he came as a humble King to redeem us.

Prayer: Lord Jesus our King, fill our lives with the joy of seeing you by faith as we journey through life; keep us yours until we worship you face-to-face in glory. Amen.

E.D.S.

For further reading, see The People's Bible commentary on Matthew, pages 23-28.

A Sad Reality

Bible Reading: Matthew 2:13-18

When Herod realized that he had been outwitted by the Magi, he was furious, and he gave orders to kill all the boys in Bethlehem and its vicinity who were two years old and under, in accordance with the time he had learned from the Magi. (Matthew 2:16)

What could you possibly say to comfort parents whose infant son was torn from their arms? How could those families ever hope to heal from such a tragic loss, being forced to hand over a child—for no other reason than to satisfy the jealousy of a deranged dictator? How do we make sense of it all? And then there is the bigger question: How could God allow this to happen?

We might find ourselves asking this question often when the news broadcasts bombard our eyes with images of destruction and loss, devastation and death. The sad reality is that, after a while, we may grow numb to suffering as one tragedy after another grabs our attention—earthquakes, hurricanes, floods, wildfires. And it always seems to get worse.

We have all been witnesses to a destructive force worse than anything that can be found in nature: sin. Isn't it true that the worst tragedies are the heartbreaks brought on by humans? Terrorism, human trafficking, exploitation, kidnapping, murder. Just like King Herod, those who commit these crimes choose to do so. How can people do this to one another? Again, how can God allow all this to happen?

We can't blame God when people do the opposite of what he commands. God reveals his will in his law—a law that can be summed up in one word: love. Love God. Love your neighbor. Herod chose to love only himself. So often we do too. Let's not ignore the devastation caused by actions that originate in our own hearts, the hurt we have caused and the damage we have done in our relationships. The reality is, if we were left alone, suffering would be all we would know for all eternity, and we couldn't blame God for what we had earned.

Satan used Herod to try to extinguish our Christmas joy, but this is why Jesus came—to conquer evil, end suffering, and slam the door on all tragedy forever. God loved a world filled with destructive sinners enough to hand over his own Son, knowing the brutality that his Son would face. That Son became an infant, vulnerable and weak, to begin a life of obedience that would cover our destructiveness with healing righteousness. He would suffer at the hands of power-hungry leaders and corrupt officials to carry out God's plan, a plan that would result in freedom and forgiveness for all who are humble in repentance and faith before him. The sad reality of life in a sinful world will soon be replaced by everlasting joy—all thanks to God's plan of salvation through Christ.

Prayer: Father, when we experience suffering and sadness, comfort us with your gospel promises of forgiveness and restoration. Remind us that we have an eternal home waiting for us; there we will be free from all evil and pain. In Jesus' name. Amen.

E.D.S.

For further reading, see The People's Bible commentary on Matthew, pages 28-32.

The Well-Pleased Parent

Bible Reading: Matthew 3:13-17

A voice from heaven said, "This is my Son, whom I love; with him I am well pleased." (Matthew 3:17)

As the cast of the production bows to the well-deserved applause, one couple in the audience cheers with a little more gusto than the others. Their daughter is the star of the musical, and they know how hard she worked to memorize lines and practice songs until every syllable was perfect. They know that she stayed up late and woke up early to spend extra time preparing, yet she still managed to complete her homework and chores around the house. They saw what no one else saw, and they are proud of her.

Children have many ways of bringing their parents joy and delight. Doting parents gush over first words or first steps, take dozens of pictures to find the right one for the Christmas card, and hang up art projects on the refrigerator. Imperfect parents celebrate the accomplishments of imperfect children so family and friends can appreciate their small victories in life.

At Jesus' baptism, the Father spoke from heaven so the world would take notice of his Son. We may be tempted to think that up to that point, Jesus hadn't really done anything yet. In some ways, Jesus' baptism was the beginning of the official work he came to do for us as our Savior. He had not performed any miracles, preached any sermons, or revealed himself at all yet—his public ministry was about to begin.

Let's not forget, though, that we needed Jesus to do more than die for us. He first had to live for us, to fight against daily temptation and win the many spiritual battles we have lost. We appreciate Jesus even more when we hear the Father express delight in his Son. Already for 30 years, Jesus had been obeying the Father's will perfectly—not a single unkind action toward anyone; zero words that needed to be taken back; and most impressive of all, not even one errant thought that crossed the line into greed, selfishness, hatred, or discontent. No, Jesus set the stage for his coming sacrifice by living a life of perfect love—without stain or blemish. Praise Jesus that when the time came for him to begin his ministry, he had a perfect resume of righteousness to offer in our place!

Here's the best part: Through Jesus, we can be confident that God delights in us as his children too. No, we haven't been anywhere near perfect. Because of Jesus, though, we are perfectly forgiven, covered in his spotless obedience. When God looks at us, righteousness is all he sees. We are God's children whom he loves, and for Jesus' sake, he is well-pleased with us!

Prayer: Jesus, thank you for living a life worthy of the Father's praise and delight, and thank you for giving that life for me. Help me live out my days in your praise and for your glory. Amen.

E.D.S.

For further reading, see The People's Bible commentary on Matthew, pages 41-44.

Satisfied by the Word

Bible Reading: Matthew 4:1-17

Jesus answered, "It is written: 'Man shall not live on bread alone, but on every word that comes from the mouth of God.'" (Matthew 4:4)

Drinking a glass of cool water after mowing the lawn and pulling weeds; eating a popsicle on the Fourth of July; savoring a cup of hot chocolate after playing in the snow; opening the Bible during a lunch break or before going to bed—what do all these have in common?

As we read the first three examples, maybe we were feeling confident—of course we know the answer! They are exactly what hits the spot, either to cool us down and quench our thirst or to warm us up when we've been out in the cold. But perhaps that final suggestion didn't hit us quite the same way. We've made it through multiple lunch breaks without our Bibles; we've gone to bed many a night without reading anything at all. Far more often, the television, computer, phone, or tablet has occupied our downtime before we dozed off. We have had either too many real-life things to worry about or too little time to open our Bibles. We've been exhausted. We've just needed time to relax. We've all made our own excuses for being too busy for God's Word.

Jesus knew better. When the devil tried to convince Jesus to use his own power to feed his body, Jesus *was* hungry. He was as human as we are, and he hadn't had a bite to eat in 40 days! And yet Jesus had a higher set of priorities. What his soul craved above all else was the Word of God. Yes, bread may have fought off hunger, at least temporarily. But when it came to battling true evil—the devil and all his temptations—only the Word would satisfy. This same Word satisfies our souls by assuring us that Jesus was victorious in this (and every) battle with Satan. Jesus fought the temptations to do what was easiest or most comfortable, all so that he could do what was holy, right, and loving even toward a world of sinful people.

He did it all for us. We need to hear the Word often—the Word of God that speaks in his law to expose our constant need for forgiveness; the Word that speaks in the gospel to show us how much God loves us, that he would sacrifice his own Son to rescue us from the guilt we piled up with our selfish priorities and our failures to fight temptation. What satisfies our souls with rest, quenches our thirst for forgiveness, and is always exactly what we need? Only the Word of God.

Prayer: Lord Jesus, thank you for defeating temptation on our behalf. Strengthen us and satisfy our souls as you work through your Word in our lives. Amen.

E.D.S.

For further reading, see The People's Bible commentary on Matthew, pages 45-57.

Disciples Keep Learning

Bible Reading: Matthew 5:1-12

When Jesus saw the crowds, he went up on a mountainside and sat down. His disciples came to him, [2] and he began to teach them. (Matthew 5:1-2)

What does it mean to be a disciple of Jesus? Maybe we hear the word *disciple* and think of the Twelve—perhaps we can remember all their names, or perhaps only the most memorable come to mind. In the previous chapter of Matthew's gospel, we learned that Jesus had begun his public ministry and had started calling his first followers. Once word got out about the miracles he was doing (healing every sort of disease and driving out demons), crowds began to gather. What drew the crowds to Jesus? For some it must have been the hope of a miracle, for others it surely was a deep curiosity just in case he might be the Messiah, and undoubtedly some stragglers simply wanted to know where everyone else was going. It's possible that people today have similar reasons for exploring Christianity.

In Jesus' day, people would attach themselves to certain rabbis and commit to following those leaders for an extended period of time in order to absorb their teachings. So it isn't unusual that Jesus quickly developed a following. However, those who came, saw, and left could not be considered disciples.

How blessed we are to join so many throughout history who have been drawn by the Spirit to Jesus and his teachings. As we examine Jesus' Sermon on the Mount, we will quickly see that Jesus' teaching is unique. He doesn't merely tell us how to do better or even give us an example to follow. That isn't his purpose. No, instead he exposes the flaws in our thinking and our living. He convinces us that the world's way of thinking is a big lie. He convicts us of sins we may have forgotten—or were never even aware of. He highlights the most critical element of our existence: our need for forgiveness and freedom from guilt.

Jesus, our teacher, is honest with us. He reveals the way God sees things; he opens our eyes to recognize our sorry state, God's unquenchable desire for holiness, and the blessings of obedience. As we learn from him, we take to heart that he is not only calling for our commitment to him but is also expressing his everlasting commitment to us. His love for us took him to the cross where he earned life for us. His love urges us to cling to his every word, to soak up his pure and faithful teaching, and to live according to it with sincere gratitude. His promises invite and encourage us to keep learning from him throughout our lives until we rejoice with him in heaven.

Prayer: Jesus, our teacher and Savior, fill us with your truth and give us the grace to keep learning from you in humble obedience. Guide us in your truth to the blessings you promise. Amen.

E.D.S.

For further reading, see The People's Bible commentary on Matthew, pages 61-68.

Filled With Righteousness

Bible Reading: Matthew 5:1-12

"Blessed are those who hunger and thirst for righteousness, for they will be filled." (Matthew 5:6)

What are you hungry for? Some of us admittedly battle a sweet tooth. Others crave something salty and crunchy. After years of discipline and dieting, soup and a salad might well whet the appetite. Sometimes, though, only a perfectly seared steak will do.

As Jesus introduced his Sermon on the Mount, he pronounced a blessing on those who hunger for righteousness. He knew the spiritual danger that faced those with only a half-hearted appetite. He knew that apart from him and his Word, we are starving spiritually.

To be sure, Satan holds out inviting but empty substitutes. Instead of confessing our sins and turning to our Savior, the devil prompts excuses for us to justify our godless words and behavior: "They started it!" "Everyone else is doing it!" "It felt so natural." "It seemed like the right thing to do at the time." Even when we recognize a failure or a missed opportunity, our adversary suggests that we'll be fine if we do better next time or put forth a little extra effort to cover up the bad with a little extra good. It's the equivalent of skipping regular meals and filling up on candy—except with eternal implications. We get a false sense of satisfaction, because there is no real nutrition.

So Jesus calls to us as our divine dietician and breaks the news we need to hear. We don't need to make a slight adjustment, try a little harder, or do a little better. We need him. We cannot be or become righteous through our own efforts; we need his righteousness to cover our guilt and disgrace, to satisfy and make us whole. We dare not seek any substitutes—only the One who sacrificed himself as a substitute for us, giving his life so that we might live eternally.

The good news is that when we turn to Jesus in our emptiness, he promises that we will be filled. When we are spiritually starving, he is the feast for us to enjoy. The main course of forgiveness comes with side dishes of comfort, hope, and joy; we drink deeply of his grace and mercy and have perfect peace as our dessert.

What are you hungry for? Blessed are those who hunger and thirst for righteousness through Christ. They will be filled.

Prayer: Holy Spirit, continually work in us a hunger that is fully satisfied only in Jesus and his righteousness. Ever increase our appetite for Word and sacrament, and bring us to the heavenly feast that awaits. Amen.

E.D.S.

For further reading, see The People's Bible commentary on Matthew, pages 61-68.

Rejoice in Our Reward

Bible Reading: Matthew 5:1-12

"Blessed are you when people insult you, persecute you and falsely say all kinds of evil against you because of me. 12 Rejoice and be glad, because great is your reward in heaven, for in the same way they persecuted the prophets who were before you." (Matthew 5:11-12)

What kinds of rewards have you earned in your life so far? In competitions involving sports or music, perhaps you have won ribbons or medals or trophies. After a theater performance, perhaps a bouquet of flowers. For doing a good job at work, have you been rewarded with a raise or a promotion? What about for being a "good Christian"? What kinds of rewards do we get for that?

At its core, being a Christian isn't about merely being "good," of course; that's the reason for those quotation marks. Being a Christian is all about believing that we can't earn a single blessing from God. No, we know the truth: "The wages of sin is death"—that's what we have earned from our Holy God—"but the gift of God is eternal life in Christ Jesus our Lord" (Romans 6:23). Heaven is and always will be a gift for those of us who repent of our sins and trust that Jesus has earned heaven and made salvation ours through faith in him. Now we live to thank Jesus and spread his Word so that others may come to faith and enjoy heaven with us.

What can we expect for that? That everyone will thank us, give us hugs, and tell all their friends to listen to what we have to say? When God works as only he can, some will believe, yes. But others? They will insult us, persecute us, and say all kinds of evil against us. We will be doing what Jesus has equipped us and sent us out to do, and *that* is our reward? And we are supposed to rejoice and be glad when it happens?

Yes and no. Jesus reminds us that human acceptance isn't what we are striving for. We aren't even aiming for God's acceptance. Why not? Because in Christ, we already have God's acceptance! We already have the reward that Jesus earned for us with his life—the only human life that has ever truly been good enough to meet God's holy standards. Jesus faced insults, persecution, and evil head-on. He earned heaven for us by his blessed sacrifice, and then in his resurrection he handed the trophy to us. This everlasting reward of grace is waiting for us, and no one can take it away. That's why we rejoice; that's why we face insults and hardships.

Prayer: Jesus, strengthen us to be your bold witnesses, confident that your gracious reward is ours. Amen.

E.D.S.

For further reading, see The People's Bible commentary on Matthew, pages 61-68.

Fulfillment of the Law

Bible Reading: Matthew 5:17-20

"Do not think that I have come to abolish the Law or the Prophets; I have not come to abolish them but to fulfill them." (Matthew 5:17)

When was the last time you fulfilled a law? That shouldn't be too difficult to answer. Even average people follow most of the rules. We stop for red lights and go on green. We pay our taxes on time. We keep quiet in the library. We stand in lines and wait our turn. The list could seemingly go on forever. Even if we don't always like the rules, we follow most of them because we would rather not deal with the consequences of breaking them.

Is that what Jesus meant here? Throughout the gospels, Jesus regularly faced accusations that he was breaking the rules: healing people on the Sabbath, looking the other way when his disciples didn't properly wash their hands, eating instead of fasting, and more. The Pharisees and teachers tried to discredit Jesus and his message by pointing out all the ways he seemed to be skirting the law and doing as he pleased. In reality, the entire time Jesus *was* doing what pleased God. And his goal wasn't to avoid consequences. It wasn't to look good and win the praise of humans. It wasn't even to be in line with the rules that humans made up. His goal was always to do exactly what we needed him to do for our salvation.

Every word that Jesus spoke was meant to draw people to God. Every action demonstrated perfect love for God and neighbor. Every thought was in line with his purpose as our perfect substitute so that his righteousness could be ours. Every moment of our lives as children of God is an opportunity for us to live out our callings in thankful service to him. We have the greatest of all reasons to do God's will: not because we hope to be good enough to get to heaven but because it is already ours. Our obedience isn't merely an attempt to avoid negative consequences. No, it flows from faith that Jesus has fulfilled everything written about him by the prophets; he fulfilled the entire law of God for us.

Obedience isn't automatic for us; we constantly struggle against our own sinful flesh, which is lawless on its own. Because Jesus perfectly fulfilled God's law for us, we look forward to leaving disobedience behind once and for all and look forward to loving God and one another perfectly forever—just the way Jesus loves us.

Prayer: Jesus, thank you for fulfilling the entire law for me. Strengthen me so that I may keep God's law out of eternal appreciation. Amen.

E.D.S.

For further reading, see The People's Bible commentary on Matthew, pages 70-73.

But I Tell You . . .

Bible Reading: Matthew 5:21-26

"You have heard that it was said to the people long ago, 'You shall not murder, and anyone who murders will be subject to judgment.' 22 But I tell you that anyone who is angry with a brother or sister will be subject to judgment." (Matthew 5:21-22)

How many of us remember being disciplined as children? Most of the time we knew deep down that we deserved discipline, but we often tried to weasel our way out anyway. "He started it," we'd say, as if that somehow absolved us of our responsibility for our own actions. Our parents or teachers could see that one coming because they were kids once too. They were always ready to respond, reminding us that we shouldn't make excuses; rather, we should be sorry (saying it convincingly) and do better next time.

Each of us has a sinful nature that refuses to grow up, won't learn from mistakes, and gets more and more stubborn each time we are disciplined. To be sure, anger is the appropriate reaction to sin—after all, God tells us of the wrath that every sin provokes in him. At the same time, we dare not presume that we have the right to lash out in anger as if it were our job to be God. God's anger is righteous; ours is seldom so. God's anger is matched by perfect love; ours so often comes from a self-centered lack of love. If we suffer, our sinful nature wants to cause pain to hurt the ones who hurt us. Our anger is murderous sin, whether we act upon it or not.

"But I didn't do anything!" We probably tried that line too as kids (although sometimes we were ignoring the truth). A similar excuse gets us nowhere with God. He can read the script that plays in our hearts—the anger there betrays us and condemns us. Only his love stops us. It leads us to repent of our anger and be reconciled to God and our neighbor in love.

All praise to Jesus, because he didn't merely preach these words—he lived them! He could have argued, justifiably, with so many who rejected him, but instead he died for all. He could have cut us off from God in anger, but he suffered God's righteous wrath for our sins and paid the penalty for everyone. He didn't claim innocence. He took our guilt upon himself, having done everything required of us. He kept God's law from top to bottom and erased our record of wrongs. Now we live in him and learn from him, watching out for the danger anger poses in our lives.

Prayer: Lord Jesus, forgive me for my anger and fill me with your love. Amen.

E.D.S.

For further reading, see The People's Bible commentary on Matthew, pages 73-75.

Is Jesus Serious?

Bible Reading: Matthew 5:27-30

"If your right eye causes you to stumble, gouge it out and throw it away. It is better for you to lose one part of your body than for your whole body to be thrown into hell. [30] And if your right hand causes you to stumble, cut it off and throw it away. It is better for you to lose one part of your body than for your whole body to go into hell." (Matthew 5:29-30)

As Jesus preaches his way through the commandments, he grabs our attention with this strong statement. Can you imagine if we Christians took Jesus' words literally and started mutilating and maiming ourselves every time we fell into sin? Where would it end? Is a sinner less likely to sin with one eye than with two? Would I sin less with one hand than I do with both of them? If we play it out, we can only imagine what a church service would look like after all the amputations and surgeries for honest people who recognize even a small percentage of the faults we all have.

Is Jesus serious here? Of course he is, although he is not advocating for self-mutilation. Consider which is more likely to be the bigger problem in our spiritual lives—that we take our sin too seriously or not seriously enough? Do we go along with the world and do our best to minimize, excuse, or redefine sin? Are we tempted to believe that whatever makes us happy at the time must be okay? Do we forget the eternal consequences of sinful choices or think we can take advantage of forgiveness by sinning rebelliously without putting up a fight at all? The truth is, if we were to cut out all the parts of ourselves that cause us to stumble, we'd be left with no heart and no mind. All sin is serious, and Jesus wants us to know it. We need salvation, not surgery.

So what are we to take away from these serious words of Jesus? As God's children, for whom the Father sacrificed his own beloved Son, we are called to battle against sin instead of ignoring it as if it is harmless. God's goal for us is everlasting life with him, and he doesn't want anything to get in the way. We can all look at how we entertain ourselves and spend our time, the friendships and associations we make and the habits we form, and we can cut out any activity that threatens to harm our souls. A temporary thrill is not worth losing out on the eternity our Savior won for us. Instead, we learn from Jesus to know the seriousness of our sin, confess our failures, rejoice in his generous forgiveness, and pray for the strength to battle on.

Prayer: Lord Jesus, thank you for suffering for my sin. Help me fight the temptations that face me today. Amen.

E.D.S.

For further reading, see The People's Bible commentary on Matthew, pages 75-77.

Yes or No

Bible Reading: Matthew 5:33-37

"All you need to say is simply 'Yes' or 'No'; anything beyond this comes from the evil one." (Matthew 5:37)

How can you expect people to trust you? You try to explain what happened, but it seems no one is buying it. They don't believe that it happened or that it happened again. You've done your best to relay the course of events exactly as they occurred, without much exaggeration at all. Still, the looks you are getting suggest that people are questioning your ability to tell the truth. The temptation (or maybe even the habit) is to add those two little words that are supposed to cement your trustworthiness: "I swear!"

Swearing may seem to be one of those harmless little offenses, but Jesus makes it clear that children of God ought to steer clear.

Swearing can be downright dangerous when the temptation arises to make a vow about future events not entirely within our control. In those cases, we might call God as a witness against himself and find out that our vow gets in the way of his promise. This can result in one of those bad situations where the truth is at stake, and it is too late to back out. (Consider Saul's oath in 1 Samuel chapter 14 or Jephthah's vow in Judges chapter 11.) We dare not bind ourselves to a course of action that is uncertain and, in the process, presume to bind God as a witness or judge.

Words matter. How did Satan deceive Adam and Eve? Simply by speaking—and much of what he said was true. Ever since the fall, this world has known suffering, pain, and death because our first parents weighed the devil's words and concluded that no great harm could come to them if they agreed to his clever arguments against God. And yet God came down and spoke a Word of promise that has the power to forgive sins, rescue from death, and free all who believe from suffering and pain forever. This Word is ours to hear, learn, trust, and share. God has entrusted his reputation to all who know and believe it; only his truth can save.

How can you expect people to trust you when you share God's Word? Every word we speak has an impact on our trustworthiness; may God help us be trustworthy in all our dealings with one another so that our words matter. Don't swear falsely, needlessly, or foolishly; don't swear at all unless required by law to do so. Consider every word vital in service to God's Word and its spread.

Prayer: Father, forgive us for words carelessly spoken. Let your Word take root in us and bear eternal fruit for you. Amen.

E.D.S.

For further reading, see The People's Bible commentary on Matthew, pages 79-80.

For Me, for Them, or for God?

Bible Reading: Matthew 5:38-42

"Give to the one who asks you, and do not turn away from the one who wants to borrow from you." (Matthew 5:42)

Imagine a bank that gave away money without charging interest. Better yet, imagine a bank that gave freely without expecting loans to be paid back at all! Word travels quickly, so it wouldn't be long before it became the most popular bank in town. It wouldn't be much longer until it ran out of money and would have to shut down. What a horrible business model! Yet Jesus encourages us to live this very same way.

As we read through Jesus' Sermon on the Mount, we might be surprised at how many of his phrases have made their way into popular vocabulary. We might hear someone who is praised for being generous and kind as the type of person who would give the shirt off his back. Great customer service is often compared to going the extra mile. If we notice and appreciate when other people act this way, why don't we all follow suit and do the same?

Jesus knows that each of us has a sinful heart that far too often gets in the way. We each hear the little voice that asks, "What's in it for me?" before we help someone else. That same voice urges us to make decisions that will allow us to have more instead of share more. Such a "me first" attitude leads to the kind of thinking that disregards God's will and ignores the needs of our neighbors. We can come up with excuses for our sins, but that doesn't make them any less sinful.

What if we lived first for God? Wouldn't we trust him enough to replace what we might give away? Wouldn't we elevate our neighbors' needs over our abundance? Wouldn't we stop asking, "What's in it for me?" and start with "Why has God blessed me with so much, if not to share with the people around me?"

Or, better yet, we could start with "What has God already done for me?" and then open our eyes to the eternal blessings that God has so freely given us in Christ, gifts so bounteous that they make any amount of earthly riches pale in comparison. Each eternal blessing is forever secured by the forgiveness Jesus won and the faith that the Spirit planted within us. We, in turn, have the privilege of using every earthly gift in service to the God who is so generous to us.

Prayer: Father, bless me with a generous heart overflowing with appreciation for your eternal gifts. Amen.

E.D.S.

For further reading, see The People's Bible commentary on Matthew, pages 80-83.

Be Perfect

Bible Reading: Matthew 5:43-48

"Be perfect, therefore, as your heavenly Father is perfect." (Matthew 5:48)

Greeting cards are often full of encouragement. "Have a Happy Birthday" and "Get Well Soon" are two of the more common wishes to be shared by sending a card; although, you may be able to find a card for just about any occasion. Sometimes receiving a card in the mail does help accomplish the wish; we all enjoy knowing that someone cares about us and is thinking about us. At the same time, the words themselves don't have any power of their own. A broken leg won't suddenly be healed by a greeting card. The card may bring a laugh or at least a smile, but it can't ensure the recipient will have a full day without any frustration or annoyance.

What about Jesus' words here? When Jesus tells us to "be perfect" as God is perfect, does it work? Have any of us heard this encouragement and immediately decided that we would turn things around and do everything the right way? Have we turned all our bad habits into good ones? Do we become perfect by listening to Jesus?

Certainly not on our own. Throughout Matthew chapter 5, much of what Jesus has said proves that we are not perfect—not even close! In this section, Jesus has reminded us that loving our friends and those who are kind to us isn't enough; no, we are to love our enemies too! By revealing God's perfect will in his holy law, Jesus exposes how completely imperfect every one of us is, down to our deepest core. Our best efforts fall far short of the perfection God seeks and commands. All of us are completely unworthy of being anywhere near him, either now or in eternity. We don't need to be better; we don't need to try harder. We need a Savior.

The good news is that the One who preaches the Sermon on the Mount isn't merely a preacher or a teacher. His message isn't simply for us to have a happier life or to get spiritually well so that we can find our own way. He is our only way, God in the flesh who was perfect for us, as our heavenly Father is perfect; he fulfilled the law for us, not just on the surface but with a perfect heart and perfect mind. Then he gave his perfect life as a perfect sacrifice so that all who look to him can be perfect in God's sight, cleansed of every sin both now and in eternity. Through faith in Jesus, we are made perfect!

Prayer: Lord Jesus, thank you for living and dying to make me perfect. What a joy it is to know you! Amen.

E.D.S.

For further reading, see The People's Bible commentary on Matthew, pages 83-84.

How to Pray

Bible Reading: Matthew 6:5-15

"This, then, is how you should pray: 'Our Father in heaven, hallowed be your name.'" (Matthew 6:9)

How should we talk to God? Maybe sometimes when we pray, we are thinking more about ourselves and our lives than we are thinking about God. If we'd start by considering whom we are approaching, it could be overwhelming. After all, he is the almighty Creator. He is the one who rules over everything and everyone. He controls the weather, and he decides when people are born and when they die. How can we presume to have a right to talk to him? Why should he listen to us?

Jesus sets our hearts at ease. It isn't that he wants us to forget God's power, but Jesus teaches us to pray in a way that approaches God humbly yet confidently at the same time: "Our Father . . ." Are there two bolder words than those in our entire language? Does Jesus mean to say that we get to talk to God the Father the same way he does? That is exactly the point! Every time we speak these words, we ought to marvel at the privilege of prayer—that the Almighty would give us the time to speak and he promises to listen intently to every word. Not only that, but whatever we ask, he promises to answer with exactly what we ask for, unless he has something better in mind (and most of the time, he does).

Jesus knows that we can come up with our own list when we start asking for things in prayer, but if we are able to pray like Jesus, let's prioritize like Jesus too: "Hallowed be your name." We may think we have a pretty good idea of the blessings that would make us happy, but just imagine the blessings that would come from a focus on God's holy name throughout each day—the peace of knowing our Father is watching over us, guiding our steps by his Spirit, and leading us along the good paths he has chosen; the trust that all his commands have all his wisdom behind them; the certainty that we have a divine purpose to love those he leads into our lives; the desire to live each moment for him because he sent his Son to die for us. In Christ we know that all our failures to show and share his holy name have been forgiven. Each day in our time of grace is another chance to be renewed by his compassion and to serve our neighbor.

Of course, we can pray using any words we choose. But let's remember to pray like Jesus, in his holy name.

Prayer: Our Father, how blessed we are to know your love and concern for us. Teach us to always pray as Jesus did and to know that you listen to us for his sake. Amen.

E.D.S.

For further reading, see The People's Bible commentary on Matthew, pages 87-94.

Safe Deposit

Bible Reading: Matthew 6:19-24

"Store up for yourselves treasures in heaven, where moths and vermin do not destroy, and where thieves do not break in and steal. 21 For where your treasure is, there your heart will be also." (Matthew 6:20-21)

Experts say that banks are so much safer than they used to be. When the stock market crashed in 1929, anxious people rushed to their banks to withdraw cash—so many did this, in fact, that a large number of banks ran out of money and had nothing left to give their customers. A few years later, the FDIC was formed to insure bank deposits and make them safer, so even if a bank would be robbed or go out of business, the deposits would be guaranteed up to a certain amount. Still, you may hear stories of the post-Depression days when people no longer trusted banks;

instead, they stored their money in an old mattress or between the walls of their homes. These days, with most financial transactions taking place in the digital space, online security has become a major industry. When people have possessions of great value, they have to solve the problem of how to keep their things safe.

Jesus reminds us that no matter how vigilant we may be with our earthly possessions, every single one will be gone someday. Shouldn't our priorities in life reflect the joyous truth that God has given us blessings that can never be taken away? Through faith in Jesus alone, our souls will live on in heaven long after we leave our earthly goods behind; apart from Jesus, our souls would suffer in eternal torment. What can we do to protect our souls—and value the souls of the people around us as well?

Consider what lasts and remember what cannot be guaranteed. Our time and energy, our health, and all worldly wealth are temporary. However, when we spend these blessings on spiritual matters, we store up treasures in heaven. We take these gifts and use them in service to God and our neighbor, showing and sharing the love of Jesus, participating and partnering in gospel ministry, and we leave the results up to the Holy Spirit. We may not be able to see a return on our investment in this life, but we trust God to work through these blessings that he has given us. We show our Savior how much he means to us, and we show the people around us how much they mean to Jesus.

Prayer: Lord Jesus, you are our greatest treasure. Give us opportunities every day to lead others to you. Amen.

E.D.S.

For further reading, see The People's Bible commentary on Matthew, pages 95-99.

First on the List

Bible Reading: Matthew 6:25-34

"Seek first his kingdom and his righteousness, and all these things will be given to you as well." (Matthew 6:33)

Anyone who has any type of responsibility can benefit from a to-do list. We may write it out and post it somewhere to keep our tasks in front of us, or we may simply keep a tally in our heads of where we need to be at what time, what we need to accomplish each day, and how we can get ready for whatever comes next.

Whatever approach we take, the problem for most of us is that our to-do lists keep getting longer and longer.

No matter how full our to-do lists may be, Jesus tells us what ought to be right at the top and first on the list every time: Seek God's kingdom and his righteousness. One more thing to do? And we are supposed to put everything else aside to do it? Yes and no. Seeking God's kingdom doesn't mean we have to leave our homes and abandon all our other responsibilities. Quite the opposite! Instead, we take time and make the effort to acknowledge God's gracious rule over our home, our work or school assignments, and our entire lives. Without God's blessing, we have no chance of accomplishing anything; when we see all we do as a response to God's forgiveness and as an opportunity to praise him with the gifts he alone has given, then each task carries divine purpose and fulfillment. We trust that God himself has equipped us and placed us where we are, and we are empowered to serve our heavenly Father and King.

When we seek God's righteousness, we soon find that we have none of our own. He is holy, and we are the opposite. Yet we need not worry, because just as God provides all that we need for life, in Christ he provides all that we need for eternity. The doubts and fears we face for the days ahead are swallowed up by the certainty of forgiveness and the righteousness that is ours through faith in Jesus. One day all our problems will be left behind, along with the shame and guilt that weigh us down each day. The God who made and fulfilled the promise of salvation will surely take care of us as he leads us along the path of his choosing. We know where this blessed road leads, and our Father invites us to walk hand in hand with him the whole way. That's the blessing of seeking him first.

Prayer: Father, thank you for the kingdom you have made me a part of and for the righteousness that is mine through your Son. Help me seek you first and trust that everything else will be given to me as well. Amen.

E.D.S.

For further reading, see The People's Bible commentary on Matthew, pages 99-102.

Look in the Mirror

Bible Reading: Matthew 7:1-6

"You hypocrite, first take the plank out of your own eye, and then you will see clearly to remove the speck from your brother's eye." (Matthew 7:5)

We all probably have found ourselves in one of those awkward situations. We start a conversation and quickly realize that something isn't quite right—and that something could potentially embarrass the person we are talking with. Maybe the shirt buttons don't line up correctly, the collar is half-flipped in a goofy way, or—worst of all—something is stuck in his or her teeth. No matter what it is, it would take only a moment to fix and we could spare this person the the humiliation of everyone else noticing too, but we know it would be uncomfortable for him or her to hear about it. So we almost lose track of the conversation as we think to ourselves, "Should I say something, or shouldn't I?"

Our ultimate course of action may be determined by another question: "Would I want someone to tell me if the situation were reversed?" Yes, it could be uncomfortable to hear—and it might be uncomfortable to disclose—but honesty is necessary to fix the issue. The truth is, though, that the whole thing could have been prevented with a good look in the mirror.

In this world, we have plenty of opportunities to notice when our neighbors do something wrong. We are surrounded by sinners, so we shouldn't be surprised when they sin. We can't help but notice the moral flaws in our family members, coworkers, fellow students, public figures, and the people in our communities. But before we point out their errors, no matter how significant they may seem to us, Jesus urges us to take a good long look in the mirror of God's law. Our conversations about sin take on a new light when we are rightly conscious of our own need for forgiveness.

When we see our own sin clearly, we have no more room for pride or judgmentalism. We need forgiveness, and only in Christ do we have it. But forgiveness isn't only for us. Our love and appreciation for our Savior then guides us to reach out to others—not to condemn them harshly, but to share with them the humility of contrition and the joy of God's grace and forgiveness. We'd want others to do the same for us.

Prayer: Jesus, let your forgiveness move me to share your truth with others, to speak of both sin and grace. Amen.

E.D.S.

For further reading, see The People's Bible commentary on Matthew, pages 102-106.

Good Gifts, Good Giver

Bible Reading: Matthew 7:7-11

"If you, then, though you are evil, know how to give good gifts to your children, how much more will your Father in heaven give good gifts to those who ask him!" (Matthew 7:11)

Any good parent knows that sometimes it is best to say no. A little boy asks for ice cream for dinner every evening, but his parents know there are more nutritious choices that would provide a more healthful diet. A little girl asks to wear makeup to school, but her parents may suggest that she waits a few years. Good parents have the ability to think ahead, to weigh the risks of certain choices, and to decide what is best for their children.

To an even greater extent, God knows what is best for his children. He can see the past, the present, and the future all at once. He knows our individual strengths (because he gave them to us) and our weaknesses (in his wisdom he allowed those too). He knows the potential outcome of every possible response to our prayers and answers each request according to his omnipotence. Sometimes—or, in reality, often—this means that when we ask, the best response he can give us is a resounding no. It may seem like silence to us, or he may direct us along a very different path than the one we would have chosen for ourselves. We ought to fight the temptation to think stubbornly that the best gifts God can give are the ones we ask for.

But the one thing God doesn't want us to do is quit asking. Jesus tells us to ask, and we can ask boldly—there is nothing God cannot do. Jesus tells us to seek, to actively search for God and his will without giving up. Jesus tells us to knock on heaven's door, to approach our Father humbly yet confidently, clinging to every promise he has made. Jesus assures us that God will give us exactly what we ask for—unless he has something better in mind. Where does such confidence come from? Our Father has already given us the greatest gift possible: his one and only Son.

Jesus is the reason we ask boldly. Jesus is the reason we seek confidently. Jesus is the reason we knock without ceasing. Jesus is the proof that God loves us eternally and will listen to every plea, every request, every cry for help, and every confession. Through Jesus we are God's children, and God our Father knows how to give us every good gift.

Prayer: Father in heaven, we trust you to know and give us everything we need so that we can know and serve you better. Thank you for all your gifts. In Jesus' name. Amen.

E.D.S.

For further reading, see The People's Bible commentary on Matthew, pages 106-109.

Don't Follow the Crowd

Bible Reading: Matthew 7:13-14

"Enter through the narrow gate. For wide is the gate and broad is the road that leads to destruction, and many enter through it." (Matthew 7:13)

"Everyone else is doing it." "Everyone else has those." "Everyone else is wearing that brand." Maybe we can remember saying similar things. Perhaps we were defending our behavior with the excuse that we were just trying to fit in. Throughout life, we often face the pressure to conform to the people around us rather than go against the grain and choose a path less traveled. So many times it's just plain easier to go along with the crowd. We won't have to defend our decisions or explain ourselves or face much resistance at all. At least we'll have company as we go on our way.

Jesus urges us, however, to consider the outcome of such thinking. Just because something is easy doesn't make it right. Just because it's popular doesn't mean it is good for us or anyone else. Quite often, godly life choices won't be easy and they won't be popular. We will need to withstand the resistance that comes from the people around us and fight against the stubbornness of our own sinful hearts. We need to remember that our own natural desires and the influences of the world are constantly steering us on a path that leads only to everlasting destruction.

Thank God today and always that he has plucked us from the broad road to hell and lovingly placed us on a narrow road to life. We didn't choose him; he chose us and rescued us from the ignorance of unbelief to bring us into the knowledge of salvation. How could we give up these eternal blessings and forsake the narrow road in favor of the wide one? How could we abandon our place in God's family and join the worldly crowd once more? God forbid that we should ever be led astray.

How important it is, then, that we cling to the precious promises God provides and keep our focus where this narrow road leads! We must keep our eyes open, watching for and avoiding temptation in the pressure to conform. We must live lives of humble repentance, knowing our weaknesses and failures and trusting in Christ alone and his forgiveness to keep us on the narrow way. As we depend on him, we can be confident that he walks with us, leading us forward to rejoice forever in his presence. Looking ahead, we see opportunities to invite others to join us on this narrow path because there is always room for one more. May God use us to support and encourage one another along the road that leads to life.

Prayer: Lord Jesus, thank you for rescuing me from the road to destruction. Use me to introduce others to you: the Way, the Truth, and the Life. Amen.

E.D.S.

For further reading, see The People's Bible commentary on Matthew, pages 109-110.

Scary Words

Bible Reading: Matthew 7:21-23

"Not everyone who says to me, 'Lord, Lord,' will enter the kingdom of heaven, but only the one who does the will of my Father who is in heaven." (Matthew 7:21)

What are the scariest words you've ever heard? A man hears of layoffs at work and wonders if his livelihood is in jeopardy. A woman hears the word *cancer* in the doctor's office and has a hard time paying attention to whatever follows. Children are blindsided by the news that their parents are getting a divorce, leading to all kinds of uncertainty as to what their home will look like going forward. Everything changes when we hear words like *layoff, cancer,* or *divorce*—words that mean life may never be the same again.

As scary as words like those can be, Jesus shares the prospect of words far worse. They are words of judgment and condemnation that will lead to never-ending suffering for all to whom they are spoken: "I never knew you. Away from me, you evildoers!" We shudder at the mere thought of being on the receiving end of such scary words. And that's the point. They are meant to be scary; what makes it even more sobering is that Jesus has every right to speak those very words to each of us.

We want to understand Jesus' intent here, though. Is Jesus trying to remove all our hope of salvation when he gives such a stern warning? No, he loves us far too much for that. Instead, Jesus is cautioning us from practicing religion in a way that limits our interactions with him to mere lip service. Our relationship with him isn't about going where we are supposed to go and saying what we are supposed to say; our connection to him is in faith—the complete reliance that only in him are we loved, forgiven, and set free from the guilt and punishment we deserve.

Our words, then, are far from empty; they are full of conviction that he is who he claims to be and that he has done everything he promised to do as our perfect substitute. He isn't just the Savior—he's *our* Savior!

His words offer life; we can trust him and live through his grace. His words offer power; we are transformed in our will to seek and carry out God's will for our lives. His words offer forgiveness; we confess our sins and turn away from them as we turn to him for comfort and to restore us every day. His words can be scary at times, but we pay attention, heed his warnings, and cling to his promises to save us now and eternally. Every word of Jesus is spoken in love so we can be sure that we are known and loved by our Savior, who always speaks the truth.

Prayer: Lord Jesus, thank you for your loving words to us. Help us always listen and take your words to heart. Amen.

E.D.S.

For further reading, see The People's Bible commentary on Matthew, pages 111-114.

When Hearing Isn't Enough

Bible Reading: Matthew 7:24-29

"Therefore everyone who hears these words of mine and puts them into practice is like a wise man who built his house on the rock." (Matthew 7:24)

Directions are useful, but only if a person follows them. Let's say someone pulls his car over in front of your home and asks for directions to a local address. As you give step-by-step directions, he nods and even adds an occasional "okay" or "got it." Finally, he thanks you and drives off . . . in the wrong direction! How likely do you think it is that he will find the way? He heard the directions, but he didn't follow them.

Sadly, a similar situation can easily play out in our own lives. We hear God's Word, and it is exactly what we need. God shares his wisdom, his guidance, and his directions for our lives in his law. He tells us what is best for us and for the people around us—what is true and right and in line with his holy will. With his gospel he invites us to know that he has forgiven us for the times we have failed. He shows us his love and empowers us to love him in return.

Far too often, though, we veer off track. Perhaps we fall back into an addiction or give in to weakness without putting up much of a fight. Maybe someone so angers or disappoints us that our emotions overrule our good intentions to be kind and patient to everyone. Sometimes we get caught up in the pressures to fit in with the people around us and end up compromising what we know is right.

Hearing the words is not enough. Jesus emphasized that by telling the story of two builders, a wise one and a foolish one. They both built a house, but only the wise one built on a solid foundation. This, Jesus said, is the person who hears God's words and "puts them into practice." He listens to God's law and repents when he finds himself heading in the wrong direction. He finds comfort and strength in the gospel promises that have fortified God's people throughout the centuries. Those gospel promises inspire a love for God's Word and a desire to honor God with his life. His house (his life) is built on a solid foundation.

God forgives us for all the times we have heard his Word and have failed to put it into practice. The realization of our need for forgiveness pulls us back to hear the Word again, longing for the forgiveness that God so clearly and fully provides there. When we hear the Word, let's also pray for the power of the Holy Spirit to work in us and give us the strength to put it into practice in our lives, fighting against temptation and striving to live each moment for the Savior who gives us eternal life.

Prayer: Lord Jesus, strengthen me by your Spirit to live a life worthy of my gracious calling, putting your words into practice. Amen.

E.D.S.

For further reading, see The People's Bible commentary on Matthew, pages 114-116.

Just Say the Word

Bible Reading: Matthew 8:5-13

The centurion replied, "Lord, I do not deserve to have you come under my roof. But just say the word, and my servant will be healed." (Matthew 8:8)

At some point in life, we all get a chance to learn what power feels like. It could be on the playground in the backyard while playing follow-the-leader—and we get to lead. It may be when we are babysitting or working at the local pool as a lifeguard—and we are put in charge officially so everyone else is supposed to listen to what we say. Perhaps we work as police officers or teachers or volunteer as coaches—jobs that come with a certain amount of authority over others built in. We find out how powerful words can be when we speak and people listen.

As a commander of a hundred men, the centurion had an appreciation for the power of his commands. He spoke, and men obeyed. Yet he realized that he was in the presence of one whose words are infinitely more powerful than his own. When Jesus offered to come and heal the centurion's servant, the centurion knew that wouldn't be necessary. He trusted that even from afar, whatever Jesus spoke would happen, just as when God spoke at creation and it was so. The centurion made a bold confession of his faith in Jesus and his powerful word. The centurion knew that no virus, bacteria, or illness could refuse to obey the Creator-God in the flesh.

Such a miracle overwhelms any doubts about Jesus' power. Even in his state of humiliation, Jesus gave glimpses of his eternal omnipotence as the Son of God, his control over all that exists, and his deep love and concern for human beings. God took on our humanity to rescue us from every ill and every evidence of the curse of sin in our lives. He healed diseases and even raised the dead to prove that his words not only were powerful but also were (and are) true. Jesus submitted to God's commands in our place and fulfilled his promise to rise from the dead, all so that we could look forward to a life without any sin, guilt, illness, or injury.

In the account of the centurion, Jesus healed the servant from afar. But Jesus is never far from us. We whom he loves powerfully, deeply, and eternally can trust in his every promise, knowing that he has our best interests at heart. He knows what it is like to live in a world of pain and sorrow, and he has overcome it. How blessed we are to know Jesus by faith!

Prayer: Lord Jesus, use your Word to empower our faith. Help us trust in you every day as you watch over us. Amen.

E.D.S.

For further reading, see The People's Bible commentary on Matthew, pages 119-121.

The Doctor for Sinners

Bible Reading: Matthew 9:9-13

"Go and learn what this means: 'I desire mercy, not sacrifice.' For I have not come to call the righteous, but sinners." (Matthew 9:13)

As we go through life, most of us deal with illness, aches, and pains, perhaps even serious disease. Depending on our ailments, we may be referred to doctors who have the specialty we require. A foot doctor is a podiatrist; a heart doctor is a cardiologist; a kidney doctor is a nephrologist; a doctor who specializes in treating cancer is an oncologist. As much as we'd love to go through life without having to learn those titles, when we are sick, we need to go see the right doctor.

When it comes to our spiritual life, the biggest mistake we could make is to think that we don't need a doctor. Throughout the gospels, we hear about how, generally speaking, the Pharisees lived in the lie that they could be and could remain spiritually whole by their own doing. They were quick to note the symptoms of sin in the people around them, especially in people like Matthew, who collected the taxes of his fellow Jews on behalf of the Romans (and presumably lined his own pockets in the process). When Jesus took an interest in Matthew as one of his disciples and spent time with him and his friends, the Pharisees must have thought that Jesus didn't care much about sin.

What did they miss? The wonderful truth that Jesus cares much about sinners! For all of us sinners, Jesus is the doctor we need. All who know the truth about our spiritual illness (the Bible points out that on our own we are spiritually dead!) know that we desperately need a doctor. Jesus is the one who can cure us. He not only *has* the medicine; he *is* the medicine. Jesus' perfect obedience is the antidote for our guilt; his perfect sacrifice is the life-giving transfusion of righteousness into our souls; his resurrection is the heart transplant we need and the vaccine against death and hell. A daily dose of repentance does our souls a great deal of good as we consult with the doctor who heals us with a full infusion of forgiveness and boosts our power to fight temptation for one more day.

What a blessing for us to see this case study of what a good doctor can do. Jesus called Matthew to follow him and gave him a whole new purpose in life. Matthew left his tax booth behind and interned with the doctor who would empower him to call other sinners. He even wrote the gospel account that serves as a basis for this series of devotions. May Jesus' love for sinners give us new purpose as well!

Prayer: Great Physician, apart from you I am terminally ill. Heal me and infuse me with the purpose you choose for my life. Amen.

E.D.S.

For further reading, see The People's Bible commentary on Matthew, pages 131-134.

Ask for Workers

Bible Reading: Matthew 9:35-38

"Ask the Lord of the harvest, therefore, to send out workers into his harvest field." (Matthew 9:38)

We don't always think of how important they are, but whenever we go to a public place, we expect workers to be there. When we go to school, we assume we'll have a teacher in the front of the room. When we go to a restaurant, someone is supposed to be there taking our orders and preparing the food. If there is an emergency and we dial 911, we need someone to answer and respond quickly. And if we drive by ripe fields of grain or ripe orchards of fruit, we expect someone to come along to harvest the crops.

Every now and then, something disrupts this work cycle that we might often take for granted. Maybe the teachers go on strike. Perhaps the chef is ill. Storms put harvesters behind schedule so they don't get to the fields in time. At best it may be an inconvenience or a temporary disruption; at worst it can mean the loss of income, the loss of a job, the end of a particular business in bankruptcy, or even the loss of life.

As Jesus surveyed society, he saw the potential for a far greater tragedy. Imagine coming to church and not having a pastor—no one to preach and teach God's Word, no one to distribute the Lord's Supper or baptize a child, no one to comfort the grieving or visit the sick or counsel those who need guidance. "The harvest is plentiful but the workers are few," Jesus said (9:37).

Now, it's important to know that pastors aren't the only ones who are able to share God's Word, administer the sacraments, or provide support and encouragement to people who need it. In fact, the harvest is too plentiful to leave the work to such a small number of workers. We all need to ask ourselves what our roles may be in the work of the church, whether that means volunteering our time, being generous with financial support, or encouraging called workers every chance we get. We can all keep an eye out for young people who would make good preachers, teachers, musicians, and lay leaders, and then encourage them to consider using their gifts in ministry. The whole time, let's pray as Jesus directs us, asking God to provide needed workers in this most critical area of life—those who will have an impact long after our lives here are over.

Prayer: Lord of the church, prepare us all for the work you would have us do. Continue to raise up faithful ministers to serve your people with the Word and sacrament. Amen.

E.D.S.

For further reading, see The People's Bible commentary on Matthew, pages 140-142.

It's Free!

Bible Reading: Matthew 10:5-16

"Heal the sick, raise the dead, cleanse those who have leprosy, drive out demons. Freely you have received; freely give." (Matthew 10:8)

Most people love a good deal. It can be a welcome surprise to find out that something you planned to buy is on sale: 20, 30, 40, even 50 percent off! It can make your whole day as a parent when you need school shoes for the kids and you find a store with a "buy one, get one free" sale happening. But we all know that there is something even better than a good sale—when that item is free!

Free happens so rarely that we question when we see such an offer. If something is free, it must be broken or defective or have a mysterious but awful smell to it. The fine print must say that the "free gift" comes with an expensive subscription or at least a high-priced shipping and handling fee. Most of the time, our suspicion is well-founded; businesses can't afford to lose money by giving things away, so usually an offer of free is too good to be true.

In the same way, people tend to think that heaven has a cost associated with it. We must have to do something, right? In fact, every religion in the world besides biblical Christianity teaches that way to eternal life—that heaven (or paradise or nirvana or a better reincarnation) depends on obedience to a set of rules. You have to give something up or pile up good works or donate to every good cause. To be fair, on the one hand, heaven isn't cheap; on the other, it's absolutely free!

How can both be true? Consider this comparison: When we were children, how much did we pay to cover the rent or the mortgage? Most of us never saw the bills until we moved out on our own or went off to college. We lived for free, but that doesn't mean it didn't cost anything at all. It was free to us because someone else—most likely our parents—worked hard to pay for it.

So it is with heaven. We are blessed, as the disciples were, not only to receive the benefit of Christ's work but also to share it. We have received the amazing news that Jesus our Savior paid the high cost for our eternal life when he shed his lifeblood and died to take away the sin of the world. He loved us so much that he paid the full price and then offers us what he earned, and he doesn't require a single payment in return. We simply trust that he has done it all to make us his now and forever, and we look for opportunities to share with others: "It's free!"

Prayer: Jesus, we never could have bought the salvation that you give for free. Help us treasure and share this good news. Amen.

E.D.S.

For further reading, see The People's Bible commentary on Matthew, pages 147-153.

Healthy Fear

Bible Reading: Matthew 10:26-31

"Do not be afraid of those who kill the body but cannot kill the soul. Rather, be afraid of the One who can destroy both soul and body in hell." (Matthew 10:28)

A friend of mine tells the story of the first time he went deer hunting with his dad. The moment came when his father handed him the rifle, and the boy knew it was loaded. Immediately my friend had a sense of awe unlike anything he had ever felt before. Like most children, he had always been taught to leave guns alone; after all, if handled improperly, firearms can be dangerous. But at that moment he was holding one in his hands, and its whole purpose was to take the life of an animal quickly and humanely with a well-placed shot; poor shooting would be a miss or (even worse) lead to a wounded deer. But there was also another perspective: The rifle could also be used to sustain life by providing food for the family. All these thoughts ran through the boy's mind, and he realized the great responsibility he had with a firearm in his hands.

How are we to feel when we remember that God alone has the power to give life and take it away? Or, even more important, that God is the one who decides whether we spend forever in either heaven or hell—the two absolute extremes of eternal existence? By his judgment, every individual of all time will either know complete joy or the worst possible suffering—and in each case, it will never end. Should this not fill us with a sense of awe and respect toward God that sets our every priority, guides our every decision, and stays at the forefront of all our thinking?

It should, but often it doesn't. Too often we get distracted by the near term, the here and now, the immediate effect, rather than the everlasting consequence. We are tempted to worry so much about how the people around us will react to us. We too easily bow to the pressure of fear—fear of not being accepted or not being approved of or not fitting in. Throughout history, Christians in various parts of the world have been concerned about physical persecution, including imprisonment, confiscated homes, execution, or torture. The very thought of such suffering here and now can cloud our focus on eternity.

So Jesus warns his disciples of all time to maintain a healthy fear and respect for God. No matter what people threaten, God remains the one who decides our eternity. He was willing to send his Son to pay the ultimate price so that we could live forever with him in heaven. How foolish it would be to shrink from or abandon our faith for the sake of mere temporary comfort and thus give up God's gracious eternal gifts stored up for us in heaven. Any suffering we face as disciples of Jesus cannot take away the never-ending joy that awaits all who trust our Savior and proclaim his name.

Prayer: Jesus, give me courage to be a bold witness. Help me keep my eyes on eternity and rejoice in the heavenly victory you alone have given. Amen.

E.D.S.

For further reading, see The People's Bible commentary on Matthew, pages 155-157.

Don't Be Afraid

Bible Reading: Matthew 10:28-31

"Even the very hairs of your head are all numbered.
[31] So don't be afraid; you are worth more than many sparrows." (Matthew 10:30-31)

Cameras are everywhere these days. Not too long ago, banks were the only places with closed-circuit security cameras, but as technology advanced and became more affordable, we started seeing them in other businesses, in schools, and even in parking lots. Now many of us have wireless security cameras in and around our homes—even on our doorbells. It makes sense, doesn't it? We like to keep an eye on what is valuable to us.

God keeps a close eye on all who are valuable to him. He doesn't need cameras to keep watch over every creature he has made, and he does far more than merely watch from afar. God is intimately involved in preserving creation day by day—Jesus says that not even a single sparrow dies apart from God's knowledge and control.

Why talk about sparrows at all? It's an argument from the lesser to the greater: If God cares for these common birds and watches over them, how much more must he truly care for human beings, who are the crown of his creation! We tend to live in fear when we think we are on our own; we encounter so many situations that are out of our control, uncertain, and even dangerous. But Jesus reminds us that God is personally invested in our well-being. At any moment he could tell us the number of hairs on our heads. His omniscient (all-knowing) watchfulness never ceases; he remains focused on each one of us with laser-like precision. He never sleeps—he never even blinks!

So don't be afraid. The God who watches over us is all-knowing and all-powerful; and to top it all off, he has placed the ultimate value on each one of us. God shows us how valuable we are by what he was willing to give up for us: his own beloved Son. We need not worry that he will leave us or withhold what we need or turn away from us even for a second because in Christ we are God's beloved children, precious in his sight. We need not doubt because our Savior has conquered sin, guilt, death, and hell by his resurrection; he has overcome the world and reigns over it from God's right hand. Our eternal God—Father, Son, and Holy Spirit—is in control of every aspect of our lives and has set us free from fear to serve him joyfully. Don't be afraid!

Prayer: Loving Father, thank you for the confidence that you are always with us, always watching over us. Preserve us throughout our lives by your mercy and grace. In Jesus' name. Amen.

E.D.S.

For further reading, see The People's Bible commentary on Matthew, pages 156-157.

How to Love Best

Bible Reading: Matthew 10:37-42

"Anyone who loves their father or mother more than me is not worthy of me; anyone who loves their son or daughter more than me is not worthy of me." (Matthew 10:37)

Teachers aren't supposed to have favorite students. Parents aren't supposed to have favorite children. Unwritten rules say that everyone is to be loved as much as anyone else. After all, God loves everyone equally, so we should as well. Right? No matter what the rules may be, it seems so natural for us to play favorites, to love most those who bring us the most enjoyment or satisfaction in our relationships. Some people are harder to love than others, and perhaps we tend to love them a little less.

Now Jesus speaks words that seem awfully demanding. In order to be worthy of him, we need to love him more than anyone else, including our own family members. Imagine anyone else coming into our lives with a mandate that we love him or her more than our parents, more than our children, or more than our best friends. Our first instinct would be to shout back, "That's not how it works! You don't get to tell me how to live, whom to love, and how much."

But Jesus is different. First, he is the Son of God, so he has every right to tell us what to do and how to live. Second, and perhaps more important in this context, Jesus knows that if we love him most, we love others best. When we put Jesus first, then our love has a starting point: "We love because he first loved us" (1 John 4:19). No one has ever loved us, and no one else ever will love us, as much as he does. In his love he was willing to leave the perfection and glory of heaven to live among sinful humans in an evil world—all so that he could rescue us from sin and its every harmful consequence: guilt, pain, suffering, death, and the eternal punishment we had earned for ourselves. Not only that but he was willing to suffer and die at the hands of sinners in order to save sinners. We will never know a love greater than his.

When we keep him first, then we love the way we are loved. We avoid the temptation to love in a way that is merely people-pleasing in order to get the reaction we want; rather, we love with an intent to do and say what loved ones genuinely need. In other words, we love sacrificially instead of selfishly. The love of Jesus increases our capacity to love. So when we love Jesus most, we love others much better than we would if we placed them first—so much better than we already do.

Prayer: Lord Jesus, thank you for loving me so much. Help me love you most, and empower me to love people better. Amen.

E.D.S.

For further reading, see The People's Bible commentary on Matthew, pages 157-159.

Come to Jesus for Rest

Bible Reading: Matthew 11:25-30

"Come to me, all you who are weary and burdened, and I will give you rest." (Matthew 11:28)

Restlessness is a horrible feeling. So much to do and never enough time—you just can't relax. You have a big day ahead and could use a good night's sleep, but you have too much on your mind. Bombarded with worries, fears—or, worst of all, regrets—your brain refuses to let you find peace and quiet. Restlessness, however, doesn't always wait until we slide under our blankets and lay our heads on our pillows. Sometimes the worry chases us around all day, distracts us from being productive, and keeps us from being able to focus on a task or pay attention to a conversation. Eventually the stress becomes a burden too heavy to bear.

Neither drugs nor drink will fix the cause of our restlessness. A vacation might allow us to run from it, but we still have to come back when the downtime is over. If we could make it go away on our own, it would already be gone. But it's not, and it refuses to leave us alone, so we drag the weight of our restlessness around wherever we go.

Jesus knows well what it is like to be under pressure. Every day was a big day for him, as he needed to remain nothing short of perfect in his obedience throughout life. He never met someone who didn't need his care, concern, and compassion. He had so much to accomplish and failure wasn't an option; the fate of humanity truly rested on him.

Yet Jesus invites all of humanity to come to him. He is willing and able to provide the rest we need. He is strong enough to bear our burdens, and his level of concern is such that nothing is too big and nothing is too small for him to take on. He doesn't even shy away from our guilt and our regrets—these too he bore in his body on the cross so that we could be set entirely and eternally free. Our past need not haunt us and our future need not worry us because Jesus promises to guide us forward according to his Father's merciful direction.

How foolish we would be to refuse his offer or to forget that he is waiting to provide exactly what we need! How foolish that we often choose to remain restless rather than to come to Jesus for rest! Instead of coming to Jesus as a last resort, let's remember to walk with him and recognize his compassionate willingness to bear our burdens every day and every night. Praise Jesus, because he is never far away.

Prayer: Jesus, thank you for your gracious invitation. Lead me to answer your call by coming to you for rest. Amen.

E.D.S.

For further reading, see The People's Bible commentary on Matthew, pages 169-171.

Should We Tell or Not?

Bible Reading: Matthew 12:15-21

He warned them not to tell others about him. (Matthew 12:16)

What an odd command Jesus gives here! Don't tell anyone? Why would the Savior of the world not want people to know about him and the miraculous proof that he is the Son of God? When we read Mark's gospel account, we hear that prohibition multiple times; Matthew mentions it far less, but every time it might leave us scratching our heads a bit. Why would Jesus want people to keep his work a secret? Doesn't this warning seem to contradict the Great Commission passages at the end of the gospels, where he tells his disciples to go and tell the world?

It may seem puzzling to us because "don't tell anyone" is the opposite of what Christians have always been told. Yet, for a time, Jesus chose to keep his popularity in check. Why would he do that? The simple answer is that Jesus said this for the same reason he spoke every word: He had a very specific mission and purpose behind everything he did. In order to be our Savior, Jesus needed to fulfill every prophecy and bring to completion the plan our Father established long before creation. Ultimately, his goal wasn't merely to be a celebrity. He aimed to gather followers, not just fans. So on occasion, he managed the flow of information by urging people to keep quiet.

Was Jesus afraid of the consequences? Surely he was aware that the Jewish leaders would react swiftly and harshly once his bold claims of divinity became known. Ultimately, it would be the charge of blasphemy (claiming to be God) that would send Jesus to the cross. Still, his motivation—including the timing of it all—had nothing to do with the fear of humans and everything to do with his Father's will.

Once Jesus knew that it was time for the fulfillment of his Father's will, he kept no secrets at all; he boldly proclaimed that he was the Messiah—the promised Savior and Son of God—knowing full well the suffering and death that such a confession would bring. Through it all, whether it was time to keep quiet or time to speak up, Jesus showed his singular focus on our salvation. Everything led to his death and resurrection on our behalf. And now that he displayed his control and power in his victory over death, all restrictions on spreading the news have been taken away. It is our job in our time and place to tell the people in our lives about Jesus. We do so trusting that he will send his Spirit to change hearts and to reveal salvation and forgiveness to all who hear.

Prayer: Jesus, thank you for your perfect fulfillment of God's plan. Give me courage and opportunities to share your gospel openly and lovingly. Amen.

E.D.S.

For further reading, see The People's Bible commentary on Matthew, pages 176-179.

The Sign of Jonah

Bible Reading: Matthew 12:38-45

"As Jonah was three days and three nights in the belly of a huge fish, so the Son of Man will be three days and three nights in the heart of the earth." (Matthew 12:40)

If we're honest, we may admit that at times we wish God would give us a sign. Perhaps as we watch the world around us, everything seems to suggest that God is absent. As we listen to the people around us, we hear so many challenges to our faith. Or perhaps the voice within us questions whether our prayers are heard because it doesn't seem as if they are being answered. Because of our limited knowledge and in times of weakness, we could sure use a sign that God and his plans are trustworthy.

Today's verse reminds us that we have a sign of God's supreme faithfulness, whether we asked for it or not. Some Pharisees and teachers challenged Jesus to perform a sign that would convince them, even though Jesus had been performing miracles for some time—healing the sick and driving out demons in public for all to see. If miracles alone could convince them, surely they would have been convinced already. In their stubborn refusal to believe his words, however, they tested him again. Perhaps they were wondering if they could manipulate him into doing what they wanted and bowing to their demands.

Jesus, of course, knew that God's plan for him was more than merely to entertain, attract attention, or even momentarily provide whatever people wanted at the time. God's plan for him was to redeem, and to accomplish it, Jesus would have to outdo what might be the most unlikely (humanly speaking at least) Bible story ever written. Skeptics can't help but deny the reality of Jonah's journey, especially the part where he survived a shipwreck by spending three days inside a fish only to be spit back out on dry land.

Jesus knew that his journey led to a far greater sign, a miracle unlike anything this world had ever witnessed before. He pointed ahead to his resurrection on the third day; he would, by his own power, come back to life after being crucified and buried. Because he fulfilled this sign, one day all his doubters will be silenced and no one will be able to challenge his claims. Because Jesus rose, he assures us of eternal healing and perfect provision for all our needs. And our greatest need was and is the forgiveness of our sins and the removal of our guilt forever. Because Jesus came out of the grave, so will we and so will all our Christian loved ones to be glorified and forever healed of every imperfection. Whenever we want a sign of God's loving plans for our lives and our eternity, let's look to the sign of Jonah.

Prayer: Jesus, forgive us for all our times of doubt. Restore our faith and hope as we look to your resurrection as the only sign we need. Amen.

E.D.S.

For further reading, see The People's Bible commentary on Matthew, pages 184-186.

A Huge Harvest

Bible Reading: Matthew 13:1-23

"Still other seed fell on good soil, where it produced a crop—a hundred, sixty or thirty times what was sown." (Matthew 13:8)

This may be the favorite parable of many a pastor. The farmer goes out and spreads seeds, and even though three out of four outcomes don't seem to work, the end result is worth it: a huge harvest. Such a prospect keeps ministers motivated and reminds them to remain faithful and patient, trusting God to bless their efforts and bring about the conversion and salvation that no human can produce.

But here's the thing: This parable isn't just for pastors. If one farmer sows seed in his field and the final result is a huge harvest, think of how much more is possible when every Christian realizes that we all have our own mission field. What if we would see a soul behind every set of eyes we meet throughout the day? What if we would regularly consider the potential for planting or watering God's Word among our classmates, coworkers, and customers? What if, by our lives, we would express the truth that it isn't just the pastor's job and pray for opportunities to partner in ministry? What if we would roll up our sleeves and go to work when God answers our prayers for a friend or neighbor in need?

Of course, we wouldn't always see the rewards. Neither do farmers. No, they plow the dirt, stand back, and take a good long look—at a field of dirt. Then they plant and, once again, stare at the dirt. Even as the seeds sprout and grow, a realistic farmer acknowledges that he or she doesn't know how much of the crop will make it to the harvest. The weather will sometimes be a friend or sometimes a foe. Weeds are always a force to contend with.

Serving people with God's Word can be frustrating—even heart-wrenching—as people refuse to hear the Word that gives life or they forsake their faith along the way.

The results are up to God. That's not a bad thing; in fact, that truth fills us, feeds us, and fuels us to keep going! Like a farmer who works and waits for God to make his crops grow, we spread God's Word, trusting that the harvest is coming. How blessed we are to be children of God, longing to be gathered into heaven as part of God's abundant harvest. In the meantime, we don't know how much time we have left to work in a way that will bring many more with us. Let's get at it, and keep at it, knowing that God's harvest day is fast approaching!

Prayer: Lord Jesus, fill me with your Holy Spirit, and help me see the opportunities you give me to spread your Word in my life. Amen.

E.D.S.

For further reading, see The People's Bible commentary on Matthew, pages 188-197.

Leave It to God

Bible Reading: Matthew 13:24-30

"The servants asked him, 'Do you want us to go and pull them up?'

29 " 'No,' he answered, 'because while you are pulling the weeds, you may uproot the wheat with them.'" (Matthew 13:28-29)

"Did you hear what the neighbor said to his wife? He must not be a Christian!"

"She hasn't been to church in months—maybe years. I'm surprised she can still be a member."

"One of our students got caught stealing. God's children don't act like that."

Do we ever hear statements like these? Is it possible we have had similar thoughts ourselves as we observe the behavior of people around us?

Throughout our lives of faith, we have no doubt grown to know and appreciate God's commands; they are meant to curb sinful behavior, convict and lead sinners to repentance, and guide believers in lives of grateful appreciation for salvation. We have also come to know forgiveness by God's grace, which erases our guilt and empowers us to live in freedom and service to our neighbor. We show who we are—and whose we are—by the choices we make and the way we live.

We also know, however, that hypocrisy is a possibility. Anyone could claim to be a Christian but not have faith. Do we ever feel as though we have a mission to root out the hypocrites and point out the false Christians around us—those whose faith or behavior may not measure up to our standards? Jesus' parable addresses the misplaced desire of any who feel the urge to go hypocrite hunting, and his words point us to a better way.

First, our job isn't to judge others—and that's a good thing. Yes, we can identify the sinful behaviors and bad habits we see in others. But, if we are honest, we must admit that they could find the same in us. Only God can read hearts, and he knows all who are his. Second, we do have a joyful job already: to be ambassadors for Christ as we encourage others instead of judging them. Rather than pursuing the misguided role of rooting out hypocrites, let's pray that God uses us to humbly proclaim the message of sin and grace, a message the Spirit will use to produce a harvest of genuine faith. Rather than judging weak Christians and driving them away from the church, let's take every opportunity to build up those who struggle and help them find their purpose within the body of Christ. When we leave the judgment to God, we remember what a gift it is to serve him and love our neighbors with compassion.

Prayer: Lord Jesus, use me to reach out with your grace and forgiveness instead of judgment. Amen.

E.D.S.

For further reading, see The People's Bible commentary on Matthew, page 198.

All-In Investment

Bible Reading: Matthew 13:44-46

> **"The kingdom of heaven is like treasure hidden in a field. When a man found it, he hid it again, and then in his joy went and sold all he had and bought that field."** (Matthew 13:44)

You won't hear too many investment strategists advise clients to put all their eggs in one basket. Markets fluctuate, bubbles pop, and strange things can happen, so the safest approach is to diversify an investment portfolio in a way that grows the value slowly and steadily over time. In fact, anyone claiming to have a high-return, can't-miss type of investment should be viewed with suspicion. History shows that such individuals often turn out to be some sort of scammer.

Of course, Jesus has more important things to do than give financial advice. He is in the business of saving souls one at a time through his teaching and then nurturing his disciples in faith and wisdom. When it comes to our eternal treasures, diversification is not the right strategy. Spiritually speaking, we have real certainty only when we place all our eggs in one basket—Christ—and trust in him alone to provide spiritual riches. Everything else in this world that may receive the investment of our time and money will one day add up to nothing. The only investment that will last is the trust we place in God's singular plan of salvation through Jesus. Our wealth, our works, and our individual worthiness will not help us get one step closer to heaven; only our crucified and risen Lord could win the forgiveness that cleanses us and makes us fit for eternal life. It's no wonder that he tells us to "seek first his kingdom and his righteousness" (Matthew 6:33), since we are hopeless without him.

This righteousness through Christ is what Jesus was pointing to as he told the story of a man who found a treasure in a field. It's worth more than anything else we have. It's worth giving up everything else in order to possess it.

The people of this world beckon us to invest otherwise. We are surrounded by hucksters with promises of sudden satisfaction and easy pleasure. We feel the pressures of society to conform to secular strategies that mitigate the risk of suffering because we are disciples of Christ. We each have our own shortsighted desires to fill our stomachs, line our pockets, and pile up trinkets instead of keeping our focus on eternal treasures. We easily forget that soon everything we see will be gone; only our souls and those of the people around us will remain until the final resurrection.

How will we spend our time today? How will we spend our money tomorrow? How will we spend the rest of our lives here? Let's invest everything we have in the kingdom, knowing that for Jesus' sake alone we will spend our eternity with him and all who believe.

Prayer: Jesus, priceless treasure, guide me through life in a way that keeps my eyes fixed on you. Amen.

E.D.S.

For further reading, see The People's Bible commentary on Matthew, pages 203-205.

Jesus Caught Him

Bible Reading: Matthew 14:22-36

Immediately Jesus reached out his hand and caught [Peter]. "You of little faith," he said, "why did you doubt?" (Matthew 14:31)

Usually we don't think of getting caught as a good thing. A student gets caught looking at the test on her neighbor's desk. A child gets caught sneaking a few extra cookies between meals. An accountant gets caught adjusting the numbers to increase the profit margins. A husband gets caught with his eyes lingering on another woman. In all of these cases, the offenders would much rather have their actions go unnoticed, because when we get caught, we get in trouble.

If we had the chance to talk to Peter, however, we can be sure he'd be glad Jesus caught him. The disciples had recently seen Jesus miraculously feed more than five thousand people, though he had started with only a few loaves of bread and two fish. Soon after that, Jesus had come out to them as they were battling strong winds on the Sea of Galilee. He calmly walked across the surface of the water and, at Peter's request, invited Peter to walk on water too. At first, it worked!

Soon, however, Peter got caught looking the wrong way, just as we so often do. Perhaps we all have those moments of great faith where we feel unshakeable, confident that with God's blessing we can't be stopped. At Jesus' command, Peter walked on water—he did the seemingly impossible! Soon, however, he caught sight of the approaching waves and could feel the wind. His focus slipped from Jesus down to his own feet, and everything reverted to the way things usually work. He began to sink.

But after allowing Peter to recognize his own limitations, Jesus caught him and saved him. God's Word does the same for us. Our sinful nature would love to think we can get away with our sins. But God's law exposes our weaknesses, our failures, and the futility of our thinking we can govern our own lives. We get caught, convicted of our wrongdoing, and corrected in our thinking. Only then do we realize we are powerless to control our own eternal destiny. Thank God that Jesus reached out to us and caught us, not to punish us but to cover us with his forgiveness and rescue us with his own righteousness. When we take a do-it-yourself approach, we can only sink. Jesus catches us again and again with his Word, turns our focus to the only one who can help, and removes every doubt and fear. When he holds us tightly in his grip, we are eternally grateful that we've been caught.

Prayer: Jesus, my faith is small, and my doubts and worries are sometimes big. Hold me close to you and keep me focused with full confidence in you. Amen.

E.D.S.

For further reading, see The People's Bible commentary on Matthew, pages 216-220.

Unclean on the Inside

Bible Reading: Matthew 15:1-20

"Out of the heart come evil thoughts—murder, adultery, sexual immorality, theft, false testimony, slander." (Matthew 15:19)

Washing your hands, doctors say, is one of the best ways to prevent certain illnesses. We don't often think of how many common surfaces we touch throughout the day: Doorknobs and handles, railings in stairwells, and office fixtures all get touched by a whole lot of people who don't give it much thought. At work, at school, or on public transportation, so many places are subjected to far more human contact than cleaning. Germs are everywhere, and they are easy to pick up—so it's good to wash your hands.

What helps with prevention can't serve as a cure, however. Three days into a head cold, you can do all the handwashing you'd like, but the cold is still probably going to last another few days. If you've picked up the stomach bug that's going around at work or school, even taking a full bath won't end the nausea. Cleaning the outside of our bodies doesn't fix something that's wrong on the inside.

The religious experts in Jesus' day were deeply concerned about cleanliness—at least on the outside. They lived their lives as though sin was contagious, so they were careful to wash their hands after spending time in public places. After all, maybe an unclean person touched a surface or an object before they did. They certainly didn't want to ingest anything that would affect their own spiritual superiority.

None of us, however, can fool God into thinking we are sinless, no matter how much washing we do on the outside. Even if we had no contact at all with the outside world, sin would always have a way to find us because we are all unclean on the inside. Though we may learn some sins through our connections with others, most of the time we don't need anyone's help to figure out how to be jealous, rude, impatient, or angry—we naturally know how. It's the way we were born, already corrupted, heirs of the sin of our first parents.

The good news is that Jesus not only points out the condition; he has the cure. Better yet, he is the cure! His spotless life was transplanted into us at our baptisms, and his bleeding and dying removed our guilt forever. Only our gracious God can "cleanse [us] . . . and [we] will be clean; wash [us], and [we] will be whiter than snow." Only he can "create in [us] a pure heart" through the working of his Spirit in Word and sacrament (Psalm 51:7,10).

Prayer: Lord Jesus, forgive everything unclean in me. Purify me for your purpose, now and forever. Amen.

E.D.S.

For further reading, see The People's Bible commentary on Matthew, pages 220-227.

Great Faith

Bible Reading: Matthew 15:21-28

Then Jesus said to her, "Woman, you have great faith! Your request is granted." And her daughter was healed at that moment. (Matthew 15:28)

In many areas of life, greatness can be measured. Great financial wealth is measured by the net worth of an individual's assets. Great intelligence is measured by an IQ test or an SAT score. Great strength is measured by the amount of weight a person can lift or move at one time. Great speed is measured by a stopwatch or a radar gun.

Faith is something that is hard to measure, though it certainly can be tested. Life has a way of introducing challenges to what we think we know and what we'd love to believe as true. Every Christian is bound to go through times of testing and temptation, when our circumstances may lead us to question God's power, goodness, and love. In our weakness, we so easily turn our trust to the empty promises of the world and find ourselves feeling further and further away from a God who promised to take care of us.

In this account from Matthew chapter 15, the faith of a believing Canaanite woman was greatly tested when her daughter was possessed by a demon. She may have wondered how a powerful, good, and loving God could ever let something like this happen. When she had the opportunity to have a conversation with Jesus, however, her faith was tested, confirmed, and strengthened as she clung to the promises of God.

In our times of testing, when we or loved ones are suffering, we can feel so weak and helpless. These aren't the times to question God; these are the times God would have us cling to his promises and pray persistently, because these are the times when we realize how much we need him. We can't trust in ourselves because we aren't in control—we never were! Instead, faith becomes great when we lean on God's greatness, placing ourselves and our loved ones in his hands, knowing that he is always working for our eternal good. We boldly hold God to his promises, refusing to let go of him, and all the while we are confident that he is holding us in his gracious hands, leading us along the path of his choosing, already knowing where we'll end up forever—all thanks to Jesus. Whenever we rest in our forgiveness and the sure hope of what God has promised through Christ, our faith is great too, because the God and Savior we believe in couldn't possibly be greater. He will never leave us or forsake us because we are his children now and forever.

Prayer: Lord Jesus, thank you for the faith you have given me. Increase my trust in you as you work in my life, leading me on the path toward home. Amen.

E.D.S.

For further reading, see The People's Bible commentary on Matthew, pages 227-229.

Who Is Jesus?

Bible Reading: Matthew 16:13-20

Simon Peter answered, "You are the Messiah, the Son of the living God." (Matthew 16:16)

What do Abraham Lincoln, Martin Luther King Jr., and John F. Kennedy have in common? History tells us that each was a great man in his own right. All three are known for speaking powerful words, giving speeches that later generations still take time to read and remember. They each inspired people, worked for positive change, and achieved the pinnacle of popularity. At the same time, these three men were polarizing figures: As much as some people loved them, others hated them. So, in the end, each of these men died from an assassin's bullet.

Jesus was—and is—a polarizing figure too. As he spoke powerful words and was growing in popularity, he paused to ask his disciples what the people were saying about him. There were mixed answers. Some people confused him with John the Baptist; after all, in an age without television, they had to base their conclusions on what they heard about these preachers and their followers. Some thought he might be the fulfillment of prophecy—Malachi had foretold that Elijah would return to prepare the way for the Lord. Others thought he might be a prophet himself—he certainly claimed to be revealing a message from God to the people. In each case, we could interpret the people's views of Jesus as high praise, great compliments for a man who had grown up in the out-of-the-way region of Galilee.

Then Jesus turned the same question toward the disciples. What did the Twelve think of Jesus? We don't know if there was a thoughtful pause or if Peter instantly responded for the group, but either way, he got it right. High praise is not enough. Jesus is worthy of the highest praise because he is the Messiah, the long-awaited Savior—the Prophet, Priest, and King annointed by God to rescue humanity. Jesus is the Son of the living God in the flesh.

How could that truth possibly be polarizing? Quite simply, because there were those who rejected Jesus, even hated him. Perhaps we aren't surprised—even in our day not everyone looks at Jesus and hails him as a hero. They may consider him a prophet, a teacher, or an inspirational leader. They can't deny that he died on a cross by the actions of his enemies. But we, his disciples, build our trust on what Peter confessed: Jesus is our Messiah, the Son of the living God, crucified, risen, and ascended on high to watch over us until his return in glory. Let's boldly confess the truth about Jesus today.

Prayer: Jesus, thank you for revealing yourself to us in your Word. Strengthen our trust and lead us to share the good news of your salvation. Amen.

E.D.S.

For further reading, see The People's Bible commentary on Matthew, pages 235-240.

Listen to Him

Bible Reading: Matthew 17:1-13

While he was still speaking, a bright cloud covered them, and a voice from the cloud said, "This is my Son, whom I love; with him I am well pleased. Listen to him!" (Matthew 17:5)

"Listen up!" A coach might shout these words in a loud gymnasium as he gathers his team for a pep talk. A teacher might do the same before final announcements at the end of the day. A band director might raise his voice as his musicians tune their instruments, in an attempt to get them all on the same page to run through a classic symphony. In each case, the speaker is saying, "What comes next is important. Listen!"

On the Mount of Transfiguration, God didn't need to get anyone's attention. He already had it. Peter, James, and John must have been overwhelmed by this scene that engaged all their senses in dramatic fashion. Jesus was glowing and so were his clothes! Moses and Elijah appeared out of nowhere and spoke to their teacher as if he were an old friend. Finally, light surrounded them and they heard the almighty God himself speak: "Listen to him!"

They had heard Jesus speak on a daily basis, but they hadn't always listened. The same problem can occur in our lives too. It may be that we think we already know what Jesus is about to say. It could be that he is saying something we don't like to hear. At times it may seem that he isn't communicating with us at all. At other times his words may simply fade to noise in the background because we are distracted by all our own concerns.

Of all the ways God could have communicated salvation to us, he chose to do so through his Word. The message of the gospel tells of his love for all: his Son's work as the perfect substitute who pleased the Father on our behalf and Jesus' willing sacrifice to satisfy God's wrath upon our sinful human race. Through the Word, his Spirit works faith, forgives sins, and strengthens us for struggles ahead. We benefit when we take the time to set everything else aside and actively listen to him.

What about others? We will never win hearts by arguing or trying to intimidate people so they believe. No, it is our job to reach our neighbors and steer their hearts to the gospel the only way we are able, by humbly pleading that they listen to him. His words give life.

Prayer: Jesus, thank you for speaking through your Word. Send me your Spirit and bless me as I listen to everything you say. Amen.

E.D.S.

For further reading, see The People's Bible commentary on Matthew, pages 244-250.

A Tax-Free Life

Bible Reading: Matthew 17:24-27

When Peter came into the house, Jesus was the first to speak. "What do you think, Simon?" he asked. "From whom do the kings of the earth collect duty and taxes—from their own children or from others?"
26 "From others," Peter answered.
"Then the children are exempt," Jesus said to him.
(Matthew 17:25-26)

Have you ever met anyone who enjoys paying taxes? A child saves up 20 dollars to buy a toy that costs $19.99, only to be told that that sales tax will be more than a dollar so she doesn't have enough money. A teenager puts in two weeks of work at his new job, the whole while calculating how he will use his first paycheck. But he is disappointed to see how taxes have consumed some of his earnings. It takes a while, but eventually we get used to the idea that taxes are a part of life.

Taxes do serve a good purpose, though. In our day, taxes pay for government functions and infrastructure that society needs: police, firefighters, road and bridge repair, services for the elderly, park maintenance, and more. In Jesus' day, those who oversaw the temple in Jerusalem collected an annual tax (worth a couple of days' wages) to maintain the building and grounds. It was necessary work, and everyone who visited paid a small fee to make sure the work could be done. Whether they liked the idea or not, most people simply got used to paying the tax.

Jesus, however, used the temple tax to teach his disciples a lesson. When kings collect taxes, they don't charge their own children. He didn't mention it, but Peter might have already known that ordained rabbis (Jewish teachers) didn't have to pay the temple tax. Those in charge were able to exempt members of a chosen group from paying taxes. But what was the application for Jesus' followers?

Consider this: Temple worship belonged to God, and it was meant to provide an opportunity for knowing God's plan of salvation better. The building, the teaching, and the sacrifices that took place there were meant to point to the coming sacrifice of the Savior of the world, to forgive sins and give life to everyone in God's kingdom. No one could pay enough (taxes or otherwise) to receive the eternal grace and redemption that sinners needed. Jesus would be the one to pay the full price for everyone's salvation, the King who freely gives everlasting life and a home in his kingdom to all who believe. God loves us so much that we, his children, are exempt from paying our sin tax. We will live tax-free for all eternity.

Prayer: Jesus, thank you for paying for my place in your kingdom. Let me serve you today as I praise you for your eternal gifts to me. Amen.

E.D.S.

For further reading, see The People's Bible commentary on Matthew, pages 253-254.

God's Will and Ours

Bible Reading: Matthew 18:10-14

"In the same way your Father in heaven is not willing that any of these little ones should perish." (Matthew 18:14)

In many areas of life, we learn to deal with what might be called acceptable losses. A grocery store or restaurant has to account for some waste when food products reach their expiration dates and cannot be served or sold any longer. If you've ever painted a room, you know that it is better to have a little leftover paint, which goes to waste, than not have enough. And there will always be a small amount of paint that gets stuck on the brush or gets washed out of the pan when you're finished. In wartime, a general needs to come to grips with the fact that there will be casualties—some will be lost in battle.

What about God? Is there such a thing as an acceptable loss to him? Not when it comes to souls. To reveal the heart of God, Jesus uses the picture of a shepherd. The parable speaks of a man who owns a hundred sheep but leaves the 99 to go searching for even one that wanders off. The point is clear, and Jesus spells it out just to be sure we all understand how determined God is to rescue sinners. Every single time a sinner is brought to repentance and faith, heaven erupts with rejoicing. This is the will of God, "who wants all people to be saved" (1 Timothy 2:4). Each one of us can be assured that God delights in our repentance and our faith, even though he is the one who worked in us to accomplish the realization of his eternal grace and blessing.

In this shepherd context, however, Jesus isn't merely teaching about God's will. He is urging us to adopt the same mindset: As we interact with our family members, our neighbors, and all our acquaintances, we seek out those who also may be lost or wandering. When was the last time you set your own plans aside to reach out and encourage someone to reconnect with the Good Shepherd? When was the last time you were brave enough and determined enough to invite someone to church? When is the last time you prayed for an opportunity to share Jesus?

Remember the heart of God and how he values every soul. We who already know forgiveness now have the blessed opportunity to share it with others. God and his saints and angels rejoiced when we repented and believed; one day we'll join in the celebration as God works through our feeble efforts to rescue sinners by his grace.

Prayer: Father, thank you for sending Jesus to rescue me. Give me a heart like yours, and move me to seek out the lost. Amen.

E.D.S.

For further reading, see The People's Bible commentary on Matthew, pages 259-260.

To, Not *About*

Bible Reading: Matthew 18:15-20

"If your brother or sister sins, go and point out their fault, just between the two of you. If they listen to you, you have won them over." (Matthew 18:15)

"You'll never believe what Scotty did. He's such a jerk!" "Did you hear what Ashley said yesterday? I can't understand how anyone could be friends with her." "Don't tell anyone else, but our neighbors are getting divorced; I'm pretty sure he got caught cheating on her." When we become aware of someone else's sin, it can be hard to keep such news to ourselves. We might have an urge—or even a compulsion—to tell a friend as quickly as possible.

Matthew chapter 18 is one of the most practical chapters in the Bible. We have plenty of opportunities to notice and talk about sin. However, our Savior guides us in *how* we should talk about sin, *why* we would talk about sin, and *to whom* we should talk about sin.

Let's consider that last one first, because there Jesus is most direct: When people sin, don't go running around talking about them. That doesn't do anyone any good and likely makes us guilty of our own sins against our neighbors' reputations. Apart from rare exceptions (where someone may be in danger, for instance), sin isn't anyone else's business. The real issue is between the sinner and God, and so our job is to issue a loving call to repentance. As frightening and awkward as these conversations can be, love for our neighbors means that we first talk *to* them—not *about* them.

We already mentioned the why: Our goal isn't to expose their sin or turn others against them; no, we wish to turn sinners back to their Savior so they each know the peace of a conscience set free by the forgiveness Jesus freely won for all on the cross. So—here's the how—we humbly approach our fellow sinners without an ounce of pride and seek to make their relationship with God right again.

Perhaps this is an occasion to ask the question: If it were my sin that others noticed, how would I want them to handle it? Would I want them to go and tell everyone else and have the news spread like wildfire? Of course not. We'd all hope that they would speak to us first—calmly, lovingly, and discreetly. We'd want the chance to confess our sins, be forgiven, and apologize to anyone we've hurt. So when we find ourselves on the outside of such a situation, let's take Jesus' words to heart and reach out with love to our brothers and sisters, fellow children of God.

Prayer: Jesus, thank you for your forgiveness. Help me minister to my brothers and sisters as I have opportunity, to win people over for you. Amen.

E.D.S.

For further reading, see The People's Bible commentary on Matthew, pages 260-262.

Forgive From the Heart

Bible Reading: Matthew 18:21-35

"Forgive your brother or sister from your heart." (Matthew 18:35)

We'd all agree—in principle at least—that forgiveness is a good thing. In real life, however, forgiving someone who has caused us harm can be one of the most difficult social transactions to complete. Our hurt could be anywhere on the spectrum, from mild annoyance to serious trauma; it may be a onetime offense or a pattern of abuse. No matter the circumstances, however, Jesus urges us to forgive one another from the heart.

Forgiveness goes against everything within us; our natural inclination is to hold on to our anger and our thirst for getting even. And Jesus says we should just let it go? In a word, yes. Even if it still stings? Forgive. Even if what is broken can't be mended? Forgive. Even if others haven't apologized and may never do so? Forgive. Even if they said they would never do it again—and then they did it again? Forgive.

How is that fair? How can we ever forgive someone who hasn't earned our forgiveness? As soon as we start verbalizing questions like these, we show how much we misunderstand what Jesus is commanding here. Forgiveness isn't meant to be fair, and forgiveness is never earned. We should also know that forgiveness isn't saying, "It's no big deal," or acting like it never happened. No, it's the opposite; before any of us can forgive, we must first recognize the need for forgiveness. The need for forgiveness acknowledges that a wrong has been committed. Why, then, should we forgive?

The parable makes the point well. We forgive because we are forgiven. Our righteous God had every right to punish us severely and eternally for our great debt of sin. In love for us, he wiped out the debt completely and gave us his own righteousness instead. He made the conscious decision to turn aside his anger and his justice because his own Son paid our debt once and for all. Even our worst sins? Forgiven. Even the ones we never even realized we committed? Forgiven. Even the ones we said we'd never do again—and then we did? Forgiven. God's forgiveness fills our hearts to overflowing; out of appreciation for our forgiving God, we seek to imitate what we love best about him.

So Jesus commands us to forgive from the heart. It isn't always easy, but it is God's will for his forgiven children. Forgiveness frees us from anger's hold on us and from our selfish desire for retribution; it shows our brothers and sisters how powerfully God's forgiveness has influenced us. When we know and treasure the character and grace of our God, instead of asking, "How can I forgive?" we begin asking, "How could I not forgive, when I am so forgiven?"

Prayer: Father, forgive us our sins as we forgive those who sin against us. Amen.

E.D.S.

For further reading, see The People's Bible commentary on Matthew, pages 262-266.

Back to the Beginning

Bible Reading: Matthew 19:1-12

> **"Haven't you read," he replied, "that at the beginning the Creator 'made them male and female,'**
> **5 and said, 'For this reason a man will leave his father and mother and be united to his wife, and the two will become one flesh'?**
> **6 So they are no longer two, but one flesh. Therefore what God has joined together, let no one separate."** (Matthew 19:4-6)

"Some assembly required—instructions included," the box says, and it even has a little picture of the tools that one will need to turn the parts into the purchased item. Many an eager consumer has spurned the manual in favor of simply figuring it out on his or her own, only to reach a point where a handful of parts remain and he or she has no idea where they are supposed to go (or if they are needed at all). Or, worse yet, all the parts are used, but something still doesn't look or work right. Should the person be surprised? In the end, taking the time to understand a product's purpose and design and how the pieces fit together—then following the manufacturer's directions—is worth the time spent to achieve the desired outcome.

When Jesus was asked about divorce, he recognized that there is a better question to consider: What is marriage meant to be? In the beginning when God created marriage, it was absolutely perfect—just like everything else God made. Marriage was designed to be a perfect union of a man and a woman, a foundation for families and societies. Even though perfection was lost in the fall, strong and godly marriages still are meant to hold families and societies together. No wonder Satan and the world work so hard to distract people from God's beautiful design and purpose—and we fall for it. For this reason, divorce is such a common outcome in our day and age. Should we be surprised?

Whether we are single, married, divorced, or widowed, all of us ought to consider how we can support and strengthen the marriages around us. If we are married, let's be renewed daily in our commitment to our spouse and to our God instead of falling into the temptation to think it's all about us and our own wants. If we are planning on or even thinking of getting married at some point, let's prepare for it by considering God's beautiful design and purpose for marriage. Married or not, let's pray for those who are, that they would be blessed in their callings as a husband and a wife whom God has joined together.

Prayer: Lord Jesus, guide, direct, and empower married couples to fulfill the purpose our Father designed for them from the beginning. Amen.

E.D.S.

For further reading, see The People's Bible commentary on Matthew, pages 267-275.

A Generous Master

Bible Reading: Matthew 20:1-16

"Don't I have the right to do what I want with my own money? Or are you envious because I am generous?" (Matthew 20:15)

Have you ever felt as though you deserved more? Perhaps when awards were handed out, you felt that the top winners hadn't really earned the prizes—you worked so much harder than they did. Or on a group project in science class, everyone got an A even though one or two students did all the work. Perhaps a coworker got the promotion by taking credit for what the whole department accomplished or by patting himself on the back while schmoozing with the boss.

Can the same thing happen in our relationship with God? Sometimes we may apply the same questions to our spiritual lives, as if God is being just as unfair as people may be. Do we ever think that those of us who have been lifelong Christians ought to have spots at the front of the line when God hands out blessings? Shouldn't we have the best kinds of lives, especially compared to those who seem to be living out our dreams yet don't go to church at all or even acknowledge God's existence? If God is paying attention, doesn't it seem right that his children would be the happiest, healthiest, and wealthiest people in the world?

Jesus told a parable about workers in a vineyard. At the end of the day, all the workers received the same pay, no matter how many hours they worked. Was that fair? Didn't the ones who worked the longest deserve more than those who worked only a single hour? When the long-termers saw that the short-termers got paid as much as they did, they spoke up and voiced their frustration. They deserved more!

The parable closes with the master's response. All the money paid to all the workers was his to give. He provided for the needs of all the workers by offering them a job for the day, whether their labor was long or short. He was free to make the rules, and none of them had the right to complain. Do we get the point? God is so much more generous than the master in the parable. He freely provides for our every need—physical, spiritual, and eternal—and no amount of work on our part could ever earn a single blessing. Our existence, our purpose, and our abilities to serve all come from him as gifts—gifts that we take for granted far too often. We don't deserve anything good, but God gives to all according to his generosity. We receive our blessings best when we receive them humbly and gratefully, eternally thankful for the generosity of our Lord.

Prayer: Father, forgive me for complaining or comparing my gifts to those of others I see. Guide me to use all that I have for your glory. In Jesus' name. Amen.

E.D.S.

For further reading, see The People's Bible commentary on Matthew, pages 282-284.

A Holy Week of Fulfillment

Bible Reading: Matthew 21:1-11

This took place to fulfill what was spoken through the prophet. (Matthew 21:4)

They had waited for this their entire married lives. For 20 years they had worked hard to save money and had lived on a budget, always looking ahead to this time. Now they were getting ready to build their dream house. As the machines started clearing the lot for construction, they could almost picture themselves sitting on the front porch, sipping lemonade, and watching their yet-unborn grandchildren playing in the yard.

The next few months, however, were riddled with unforeseen circumstances. She was diagnosed with a rare illness and wasn't able to keep working in the career she had built. The contractor kept coming back with new, higher estimates. And the final cost crept beyond their budget. The neighbors complained to the city that their planned white picket fence wouldn't fit in with the architecture of the neighborhood, so they were forced to abandon it—along with a few other favored features. After the necessary cuts and revisions, the home wasn't at all what they had pictured in their minds.

We all need to set goals, make plans, and work toward them; still, our hopes aren't guaranteed—far from it! We expect some obstacles along the way, but we have no way of preparing for every possible setback. The good news is that God's plans are unstoppable. The One who made the promises is all-knowing and all-powerful. The One who fulfilled the plans was our perfect substitute, fulfilling God's law and paying the penalty for our guilt. No amount of resistance, rejection, or rebellion could stand in his way, whether it came from sinful civilians, secular authorities, or even spiritual enemies.

Everything that happened during Holy Week, no matter how unsettling it may have been to Jesus' followers, happened exactly the way God had planned it and had spoken about it through the prophets. The week started with Jesus entering Jerusalem, and there was only one way he could come in because it had been determined and detailed in the prophecy of Zechariah. "Your king comes to you, gentle and riding on a donkey" (Matthew 21:5). All who had waited for the coming Messiah may not have recognized the fulfillment at the time, but their hopes were not disappointed. Their God-given trust was rewarded as every promise came true. So too we see our Savior and King as the God-appointed Redeemer, ready and willing to give his life so that we may be part of his kingdom of grace and glory forever.

Prayer: Lord Jesus, thank you for fulfilling every promise as the world's one and only Redeemer. Draw me to a greater trust in your eternal goodness as I see each prophecy reach its perfect end. Amen.

E.D.S.

For further reading, see The People's Bible commentary on Matthew, pages 291-296.

Doubtless Faith

Bible Reading: Matthew 21:18-22

Jesus replied, "Truly I tell you, if you have faith and do not doubt, not only can you do what was done to the fig tree, but also you can say to this mountain, 'Go, throw yourself into the sea,' and it will be done.
22 If you believe, you will receive whatever you ask for in prayer." (Matthew 21:21-22)

One of the many struggles Christians face in life is that of doubt. God makes such tremendous promises to his children, promises that are meant to comfort, encourage, and strengthen our trust in him, but the world offers reasons to doubt. It's likely that at some point each of us has been disappointed when we trusted too much in a promise that failed us, when someone we relied on proved to be unfaithful. Perhaps people took advantage of our inexperience in life and lied to us to get what they wanted. Or perhaps circumstances changed and external factors kept them from fulfilling what they had guaranteed. Over time we learn that having some level of doubt is actually wiser and safer than putting all our hopes in human promises.

Do we ever struggle with doubt when Jesus makes promises to us? Are we concerned that Jesus might not be so different from all those other people who have let us down? Consider today's verses. When Jesus talks about faith having the power to wither a fig tree or transplant a mountain into the ocean, what is our first reaction? Every logical fiber within us says, "That sounds impossible, Jesus." Or, if we really have our guard up, we respond more bluntly: "I doubt it." Such skepticism regarding God's promises through Christ can have a harmful impact on our prayer life, our worship life, and our life of discipleship in general. We take more of the burden on ourselves when we aren't willing to trust fully what God has declared and affirmed to us.

If and when doubts creep in, remember the beautiful truth that our God became human, like us in every way except one—he had no sin. He was lied to, but he cannot lie. People doubted him, but he had no doubts about his mission. He faced every temptation and overcame each one to achieve a spotless life that would serve as a once-for-all sacrifice. He gave himself over to death to crush death, and his resurrection is the undeniable truth that every word he speaks is worthy of our doubtless faith. We pray in his name, and God answers for his sake. Our Lord will never let us down.

Prayer: Lord Jesus, remove my doubts and send your Spirit to strengthen my faith to be firm in you. Amen.

E.D.S.

For further reading, see The People's Bible commentary on Matthew, pages 299-302.

You Are Chosen

Bible Reading: Matthew 22:1-14

"Many are invited, but few are chosen."
(Matthew 22:14)

Can you think back to a time when you were chosen for something? Out of all those who could have been selected, they chose you—to be a team captain, to sing the solo, to be a dance partner, to take the lead on a big project for a customer, to go on a date. How special it is when anyone could have been chosen, but they picked you! Depending on the circumstances, it can be humbling, rewarding, frightening, exciting, or surprising (or some combination of those emotions). Maybe you're still waiting to find out who's been chosen for the next big opportunity, or you might still be getting over the last time you weren't chosen.

Of course, the biggest choice of all is God's; in Christ, he has chosen you. He placed his name on you at your baptism and provided you with an outfit of Jesus' righteousness to wear for time and for eternity. None of us can consider it a reward; we have no claim on having earned God's gracious invitation. If we tried to bargain our way into heaven, the divine host would see through the charade and see to it that we remain outside. If we tried to buy our way in, we'd soon find that we possess nothing of value that he doesn't already own and control. He chose us because he chose to be merciful. He chose us because he loves us for Jesus' sake.

How does this news affect our lives? Doesn't it change everything? When we look in the mirror, we may be tempted to focus on the imperfections, the regrets, the failures from which we feel we cannot escape. We are tempted at times to base our worth on the evaluation of others, and we wind up living and dying with their opinions of us.

What if we saw ourselves the way God sees us, through the lens of the cross, completely covered by Jesus? What if we considered the enormous price he was willing to pay to make us his own? Would we not see purpose and significance, value and power in ourselves as adopted children of God because our Father has chosen us to be his for eternity? Would we not be continually grateful that he has rescued us from our unproductive quest to find meaning apart from his design and his saving plan? Would we not be constantly drawn to him for our affirmation and our worth? We are chosen in Christ. Let's never forget this beautiful truth.

Prayer: Loving Father, thank you for loving me and choosing me. Build me up to serve you and my neighbor as I see new purpose for my life. Amen.

E.D.S.

For further reading, see The People's Bible commentary on Matthew, pages 309-312.

Greatness in Service

Bible Reading: Matthew 23:1-12

"The greatest among you will be your servant." (Matthew 23:11)

Doesn't it seem that the greater the amount of influence people have, the less they need to do for themselves? Try to imagine a president pushing a lawn mower and pulling weeds on the White House grounds. Picture a movie star walking along the sidewalk until she gets to the end of the red carpet because she had to park her car far away from the premiere venue. How many Fortune 500 CEOs get to the office early so they can start a pot of coffee for the lower-level workers? Each scenario seems far-fetched, doesn't it? Those who are powerful, famous, wealthy, and successful have reached a point of worldly greatness that frees them from mundane service.

Godly greatness is different. In fact, it's completely upside down from the way the world so often works. Jesus tells us that "the greatest among you will be your servant." Such a statement defies human logic. If I serve others, am I not putting aside any power and authority I have to tell them what to do? If I serve others, am I not taking the risk that it will cost me more money and time than I might gain from them? If I serve others, isn't there the chance that they will unfairly advance in life more quickly than if I simply did what was best for me?

Here's the real question, though: If I serve others, am I not living and acting the way Jesus did for me? Jesus set aside the use of his almighty power and the glory of heaven to come into this broken world and serve sinners. Jesus knew his path led to scorn, suffering, and a cross, but he was willing to pay that price—only his perfect life given into death could redeem us from eternal damnation. Jesus came not "to be served, but to serve, and to give his life as a ransom for many" (Matthew 20:28) so that we could have what we could not earn: an everlasting home in the mansions of paradise. His service is unmatched, and his greatness is beyond anything we can imagine.

When Jesus calls us to serve, he isn't ordering what we should do; no, our loving master is inviting us to know how fulfilling it can be to make a real difference for people's lives—and perhaps for their eternity! He is urging us to live as the new creations he has made us through his sacrificial service on our behalf. He is showing us the beauty of seeking godly greatness and sharing what we have received freely from the greatness of our Savior.

Prayer: Jesus, thank you for your selfless service for me. Help me see greatness in serving you and others. Amen.

E.D.S.

For further reading, see The People's Bible commentary on Matthew, pages 322-326.

Jesus Longs to Gather

Bible Reading: Matthew 23:13-39

"Jerusalem, Jerusalem, you who kill the prophets and stone those sent to you, how often I have longed to gather your children together, as a hen gathers her chicks under her wings, and you were not willing." (Matthew 23:37)

One of the most heartbreaking experiences a human can endure is to love someone dearly but receive no love in return. A young man might be infatuated with a young woman, but she doesn't even know he exists—and it hurts. However, heartbreak isn't at all limited to a romantic kind of love. Perhaps you know parents whose child has refused loving discipline and has gone off on his or her own way. All the caring mother and father want is for their child to have a good, productive life, but the child won't listen. Eventually the parents have to recognize their child's independence and hope the child learns on his or her own before it's too late. Pastors and teachers can suffer the same heartbreak when students with so much potential won't apply themselves to learning God's Word. Church leaders experience heartache when a fellow member whose relationship with the church appears to be weakening won't pick up the phone to answer or won't respond to a letter.

We are all aware of the weakness that results from sin's impact on what God designed to be perfect. The level of our physical well-being is at the mercy of whatever condition our body is in due to our age, our health, and our lifestyle choices. Just as time can take a toll on our bodies, however, our experiences can also take a toll on our emotional well-being. In the person of Jesus Christ, God became human. Jesus knew both physical and emotional pain.

At this particular moment in Matthew's account, even as Jesus knew his own death was near, he mourned the spiritual death of so many he had come to save. Some of them had wandered off on their own; others were led astray by corrupt preachers and teachers who valued a show of righteousness that fed their pride over inner purity—works over repentance and faith. Still others grew up without much godly influence at all. Of course, any of us could look around at the people we know and see plenty of examples of the same. Does such a realization affect us at all emotionally?

If we aim to be Christlike in every respect, it should. Still, let's be sure that compassion for the lost and straying isn't merely an emotional exercise. Jesus gave his very life to rescue a world of lost sinners; he didn't simply lament from afar. What can we do today to encourage, support, love, and care for souls the way Jesus did?

Prayer: Lord Jesus, use me to reach a wandering soul today. Give me courage to engage others, and bless my efforts to lead them closer to you. Amen.

E.D.S.

For further reading, see The People's Bible commentary on Matthew, pages 326-337.

Stand Firm to the End

Bible Reading: Matthew 24:1-35

"The one who stands firm to the end will be saved." (Matthew 24:13)

"Heaven and earth will pass away, but my words will never pass away." (Matthew 24:35)

"I just can't take it anymore . . . I give up." A boxer who has absorbed too many punches is unable to leave the corner for the final round, so his trainer throws in the towel. A general realizes he has lost too many troops and he is cut off from his supply lines, so it's time to negotiate terms of surrender. An aging salesman can no longer muster the energy for life on the road with all the packing, then unpacking, and reciting the same pitch for the same product over and over again, so he sets a date to retire.

As Jesus revealed the signs of the end to his disciples, he didn't pull any punches. He began, and then added to, a list of events that could overwhelm even the most confident believer: the spread of deceptive false teachers, increasing numbers of wars, famines, earthquakes—and that was just the beginning. Then Jesus listed the fierce persecution from those who would hunt down and even kill Jesus' followers simply for connection and allegiance to him.

The world hates Jesus' followers because it hates him. Sadly, Jesus warned, even many Christians will fall away and turn on one another. If we could choose, we would avoid such events, but they will all happen before Jesus returns.

How can anyone be expected to handle it all? How much can we take? Perhaps Jesus knows that we can withstand more if we aren't completely surprised by it all. In the end, he wants us to know that even though it may appear that everything is falling apart, all these difficulties will last only as long as he allows.

When we stand on his words, however, we have a firm foundation that will never pass away. Jesus' words are more certain and more permanent than the sun, moon, and stars, even the earth under our feet. We stand on his forgiveness and know that no one can accuse us. We stand on his resurrection and know that even if our lives are taken from us, he can and will restore us in a greater glory than we have ever known. We stand on his ascension and know that he will come back to this world the same way he left it.

When Jesus returns, may he find us standing firm. Sin, death, and Satan will have only one option; they are already defeated and will have to give up. The world with its corruption and disasters will be forced to throw in the towel. We stand firm in Jesus' victory already won.

Prayer: Jesus, keep me standing firm in your everlasting Word. Amen.

E.D.S.

For further reading, see The People's Bible commentary on Matthew, pages 337-353.

Be Ready

Bible Reading: Matthew 24:36-51

"So you also must be ready, because the Son of Man will come at an hour when you do not expect him." (Matthew 24:44)

An emergency room doctor can't schedule appointments. She has to be prepared that a victim of trauma or an individual suffering a heart attack could be dropped off anytime, night or day. There's no way to predict how busy a shift may be—everyone must be ready to go to work at a moment's notice. A firefighter working a 48-hour shift has to eat and sleep when he can, knowing that a meal or a nap may be interrupted if the bell rings and it's time to gear up for a call—it's crucial to be ready, or someone may face serious consequences in a critical situation.

When Jesus returns, he isn't going to call ahead and schedule an appointment. He won't give us a window of time to watch for his arrival; he declares that he will show up when nobody expects him. We are all warned to be ready for the trumpets to sound the alarm that this world is ending. If we aren't ready, we won't have a second chance; it will already be too late for anyone who isn't prepared to meet our Lord and judge. The consequences will be serious, and they will be eternal.

So here's the question: How can we possibly be ready—and stay ready—when we have no idea what day or hour Jesus will return? The good news for all who live in repentance and faith is that our readiness doesn't consist in the number of good works we could pile up or in anything we could do to sway God's standards of justice and holiness in our favor. No, our preparedness is the gift of the Holy Spirit, who has cleansed us in Baptism and planted within us the knowledge and confidence that Jesus has taken away every sin along with the guilt and damnation we had secured for ourselves. Our righteous status is secured, and though we cannot predict the timing, we have been assured of the outcome of our judgment. We need not fear our Lord's return.

Still, as we wait expectantly, we ought to make good use of the tools of readiness God has given us in the means of grace. God's Word sharpens our focus away from the distractions of this busy world and reminds us to dwell on God's promises. The Holy Supper gives us a foretaste of the heavenly banquet and strengthens our focus on the fellowship of the church. Corporate worship allows us to participate in the mutual encouragement of our brothers and sisters in Christ. Thanks to God, we are ready. Let's remain ready to meet Jesus.

Prayer: Lord Jesus, keep me ready and waiting to meet you. Amen.

E.D.S.

For further reading, see The People's Bible commentary on Matthew, pages 353-356.

Well Done

Bible Reading: Matthew 25:14-30

"His master replied, 'Well done, good and faithful servant! You have been faithful with a few things; I will put you in charge of many things. Come and share your master's happiness!'" (Matthew 25:21)

Have you ever wondered why life can seem so unfair? Maybe you've heard people talk about life as if it were one big game of chance, a lottery that is almost entirely won or lost by the time a person is born. Some babies win big because they are born into wealthy families; they grow up without ever experiencing anything but the most lavish of lifestyles. Other children are born into poverty, fighting for survival from youth throughout adulthood. Most people are somewhere in the middle of this spectrum of comfort. It can all appear to be so random.

Each of us gets only one chance at life. How awful it would be if life were one big race to the finish and the eternal outcome was determined by earthly measures: wealth, popularity, corporate success, political power, societal influence, or anything comparable. It wouldn't be fair at all, since some people are clearly born with a huge head start. Even in civilizations with a more level playing field, any competition results in more losers than winners. Perhaps Jesus' words today give us some insight for reflection.

In this parable, three servants of differing skill levels are given respective amounts of money to invest. When the master returns after a while, he rewards the servants according to one measure: whether they have wisely and faithfully used what they were given. So too, if we are truthful, we must admit that all of us were born with nothing of our own. Everything we have has been given by a gracious God—all our abilities and talents, all our health and possessions first belonged to him. Not only that but God has given us eternal blessings through Baptism, his Word, and Holy Communion—blessings that grow and multiply through our faithful use of the means of grace. Our sins are forgiven. We have peace with God. We are empowered and guided to serve our neighbor in love as a response to God's love in Christ, and we are equipped to share the gospel as we reach the lost and nurture our fellow believers. All these blessings—so much more than we fairly deserve—are gifts to and through us from our eternally faithful Father.

How do we measure up to others? That is never the right question. Instead, let's keep striving to be faithful with God's gifts—our time, our money and possessions, our abilities and talents. For Jesus' sake, a life lived in faithfulness to God is a job well done.

Prayer: Lord, help me see the gifts you have given me and move me to use them. You have saved me; let me live for your glory and praise. Amen.

E.D.S.

For further reading, see The People's Bible commentary on Matthew, pages 360-365.

The Righteous Answer

Bible Reading: Matthew 25:31-46

"Then the righteous will answer him, 'Lord, when did we see you hungry and feed you, or thirsty and give you something to drink?'" (Matthew 25:37)

Judgment day is not going to go the way most people picture it. Perhaps they imagine themselves standing in a long line, nervously awaiting their appointment to be assigned a place for eternity. As they pass the time, they may think of the times they tried hard to be good people: when they gave money to charity, when they volunteered time to help a hospital or community organization, when they woke up on Sunday morning to go sit in church for an hour or so. They may remember their worst offenses as well and hope against all hope that the good they did outweighed the bad.

On the other hand, those who know God's Word may picture things differently. We know that nothing we have done is enough to pay for the guilt we have piled up. Our sins rightly fill us with sorrow, and our only hope is in God's plan of salvation, his promise to show mercy to all who rely on the One he appointed to bear our offenses and overcome the accusations of the devil. When it comes to meeting God, we may picture ourselves falling at his feet and pleading for his grace and forgiveness to cover us, because he alone can make us worthy of his heaven.

As the King divides the sheep and the goats, however, he makes it sound as though people on both sides are surprised by what happens. Instead of demanding honor from those who believe in him, he praises them for all the works they did for him throughout their lives. Their response is beautiful! None of them step up to pat themselves on the back and respond with an "I'm glad you noticed." No, they don't even remember doing them! Their righteous answer proves that they didn't show obedience to earn anything; their works of kindness to one another were simply the natural response to God's love and forgiveness that moved them to act.

So too those who are sent away are puzzled by the King's condemnation. They act as if they never had a chance to serve Jesus in this life—because they were too busy serving themselves. The works they relied on were done only for their own praise and reward, not for anyone else—especially the Lord.

What's the point for us? As we look ahead, we can remain confident that through faith in Christ alone, we have been made worthy to share in our master's happiness forever. And until then, we have daily opportunities to serve him as we serve our neighbors: our family and friends, our coworkers or fellow students, and even complete strangers. Whatever we do for them, we do for the One who saved us eternally.

Prayer: Jesus, thank you for living and dying for me. Strengthen my will to serve my neighbor today. Amen.

E.D.S.

For further reading, see The People's Bible commentary on Matthew, pages 365-370.

The Perfect Meal

Bible Reading: Matthew 26:17-30

While they were eating, Jesus took bread, and when he had given thanks, he broke it and gave it to his disciples, saying, "Take and eat; this is my body."
27 Then he took a cup, and when he had given thanks, he gave it to them, saying, "Drink from it, all of you.
28 This is my blood of the covenant, which is poured out for many for the forgiveness of sins."
(Matthew 26:26-28)

We each could probably name what we would consider to be our perfect meal. We could pick our favorite foods and our favorite drinks and fill the table with them—and then eat until we didn't have room for another bite. What would it look like? That's the difficulty; every individual would have his or her own ideas of what a perfect meal would be. Tastes vary. Standard diets and preferences differ widely throughout the world. Our eating experiences are so distinct that what one person craves, another person finds off-putting. Some people have a sweet tooth, others have issues with certain textures, still others have food allergies. It would be hard to imagine a restaurant with only one choice on the menu. Maybe it's also hard for us to nail down what we would choose for our perfect meal.

One thing we can say with a high degree of certainty is that if we were asked to name our choice of a perfect meal, we wouldn't use words like *body* and *blood*. Yet Jesus said, "Take and eat; this is my body. . . . Drink from it. . . . This is my blood of the covenant." We who believe the words of Jesus treasure this meal as the feast that proclaims us perfect in God's sight. This food for our souls was given and poured out for forgiveness; no matter what our taste for temptation may have been, we are personally cleansed and renewed thanks to the sacrifice our Savior made.

The bitterness of our guilt has been replaced by the sweet and lasting peace with God that he sets before us, and our cup overflows with the power to love and forgive our neighbors instead of the urge to hold any grudges or ill will against them.

This is never a meal for one, though. When we take part in this miraculous meal, we are also proclaiming a unity of faith, testifying that we all agree on the hope we share and the gospel we proclaim until he comes again. At the same time, we experience a foretaste of the heavenly banquet to come, where we will enjoy perfect fellowship with forgiven sinners like us from every age of humanity—from Adam and Eve to those who are still alive to meet Jesus when the final trumpet sounds. This Supper is indeed the perfect meal!

Prayer: Lord Jesus, thank you for feeding your church with your Holy Supper. You satisfy our souls with your everlasting forgiveness. Amen.

E.D.S.

For further reading, see The People's Bible commentary on Matthew, pages 379-385.

As God Wills

Bible Reading: Matthew 26:36-46

Going a little farther, he fell with his face to the ground and prayed, "My Father, if it is possible, may this cup be taken from me. Yet not as I will, but as you will." (Matthew 26:39)

Maybe by now we have learned from Jesus' example, and we echo his prayer in our own. It may go something like this: "God, here's what I really want (perhaps a health improvement, a new job opportunity, a victory in a sports contest, a high grade point average, etc.), but if you have other plans, I'll find a way to be okay with that." Every time we join in the Lord's Prayer, we include the petition "Your will be done on earth as it is in heaven." How do we understand these words we speak to God?

Consider Jesus in the garden. Once again we note the difficulty of his being true God and true man in one person. On the one hand, he was completely aware of the rejection, the pain and suffering, and the death and burial that lay ahead of him over the next 24 hours; it was God's eternal plan. On the other hand, he had to wrestle with his human instinct to avoid pain and consider his own survival. Without refusing the mission he had been given (and perhaps more for our good than his own), he prayed earnestly to see if salvation could be won in any other way. Might there be an alternative, some other way to accomplish the same goal without the great personal anguish and torture to come? "Yet not as I will, but as you will."

Was Jesus lowering his expectations of the Father or admitting that even his most sincere prayers might not be heard? Of course not. Jesus was trusting his Father entirely to decide on the best possible outcome. If the crucifixion was the only way to save sinners, then that's what Jesus wanted most. He trusted that his Father's plans were the best of all, and so he prayed for the Father's will to be done.

And so do we. When we ask for God's will to be done in our lives, we aren't giving God permission to do something less than we ask; we are trusting that he can and will do more than we ask! Sometimes our prayers align with God's will and he gives us exactly what we pray for. At other times God's will is so much better than ours that his response to our prayers is something we didn't have the wisdom even to consider. The proof of his love is that he gave us forgiveness and life by the only way possible—the selfless sacrifice of his own Son in our place. How could such a giving God do anything but what is eternally best for us?

Prayer: Father, thank you for hearing my prayers and answering them according to your gracious will to bless and save me. Amen.

E.D.S.

For further reading, see The People's Bible commentary on Matthew, pages 387-391.

Fulfilled This Way

Bible Reading: Matthew 26:47-56

"Do you think I cannot call on my Father, and he will at once put at my disposal more than twelve legions of angels? 54 But how then would the Scriptures be fulfilled that say it must happen in this way?" (Matthew 26:53-54)

Have you ever made a prediction that hit the mark almost perfectly? Perhaps you guessed how well you did on a test, what the final score of a sporting event would be, or what the temperature was outside. You may have been within a point or two; if you were extremely lucky, you may have even guessed the exact number correctly.

Of course, your guesses may have been well-informed. For instance, for the test, you probably studied well enough to know which questions you answered correctly and which ones you hadn't prepared for. You might have had some well-informed perspective on statistics and matchups that provided data for your game prediction. Perhaps you were paying attention to weather patterns and indicators, and that put you in the right ballpark for the temperature forecast. But in the end, these events were entirely out of your control. You made some observations and then, based on what you learned, you offered your predictions.

When Jesus was arrested, his disciples considered their chances of being able to protect him; Peter even lashed out with his dagger to prevent the mob from getting any closer. However, instead of encouraging or thanking them for the effort, Jesus told them to stand down. He had far more powerful allies to employ—thousands of angels stood ready to intervene, if necessary. But Jesus didn't call on them to take up arms. Why not (and what does this have to do with us)?

Jesus' focus was not on his own safety, so he did not resist. In fact, for the age-old prophecies to be fulfilled, he had to be bound and put on trial, sentenced, and crucified. Such was the cost of the world's redemption. Jesus was in perfect control, and yet he made himself vulnerable, arrestable, and killable, all so that we would be rescued from the torment, punishment, and death we deserved. What a merciful act of love as well as a demonstration of his power to direct all history in order to accomplish the Father's singular plan to save sinners!

Matthew's record is yet another example of perfect prediction and fulfillment. Jesus couldn't have become our Savior if he had merely been close. He had to fulfill every prophecy exactly the way it was written—and he did! He was and is our perfect Redeemer. The Son of God handed himself over to sinful people to set us free from sin forever.

Prayer: Lord Jesus, thank you for going willingly to the cross for me. Only in you can I live in freedom from guilt. Amen.

E.D.S.

For further reading, see The People's Bible commentary on Matthew, pages 392-395.

No Defense

Bible Reading: Matthew 27:11-26

Jesus made no reply, not even to a single charge—to the great amazement of the governor. (Matthew 27:14)

Imagine you are accused of a horrific crime that you did not commit. The police bust down your door, handcuff you and interrogate you, and then lock you up in a cell. Weeks go by until it is time to go on trial; then a parade of witnesses for the prosecution list the "evidence" pointing to the reason you must surely be guilty and are deserving of severe punishment. When the accusations finally come to an end, the judge asks if you have anything to say in your own defense.

It's likely you would have been waiting for that moment for a long time. You'd have your alibi ready to go, along with all the reasons why it should be clear to everyone that the wrong person is on trial. After all, you're innocent! Why be punished for something you didn't do?

Now think of Jesus. He had his moment to speak, to defend himself and set the record straight, to explain to Pontius Pilate how all of this was a huge misunderstanding. Yes, Jesus had claimed to be the Son of God, but he could prove that it was true! He could have performed miracle upon miracle on demand to show his divine nature. He could have answered any question they asked. He could have given answers no one else could possibly know unless he or she had understanding from heaven itself.

Instead, Jesus made no reply. He neither denied the lies against him nor defended the truth of his innocence. Why not? He made no defense because he was willing to go through a severe punishment worse than anything that the Roman soldiers could do to him. He ignored the human injustice because his mission was divine justice: Every sin must be paid for, and only he could pay the price. If Pilate was amazed with Jesus' silence, how much more stunned he would have been if only he understood the eternal love behind it!

We have some idea of the eternal love behind it, although even we who know the outcome of the trial cannot fully comprehend why Jesus would go to such great lengths for us. Still, we are filled with confidence that when we stand before God for judgment, though we have no suitable alibi or excuse for our many sins, Jesus' blood will cry out in our defense. His righteousness fully covers our every imperfection. He remained silent so we may sing God's praises unceasingly in this life and the next. He humbly submitted to those who would crucify him so that we would have the sure hope of glorification when he calls us home to reign with him. Satan can accuse us no longer; Jesus Christ is our sure defense.

Prayer: Jesus, thank you for suffering obediently in my place. Make each day of my life a response to your love for me. Amen.

E.D.S.

For further reading, see The People's Bible commentary on Matthew, pages 407-413.

See What He Suffered!

Bible Reading: Matthew 27:27-31

**They stripped him and put a scarlet robe on him,
29 and then twisted together a crown of thorns and set
it on his head. They put a staff in his right hand. Then
they knelt in front of him and mocked him. "Hail,
king of the Jews!" they said.** (Matthew 27:28-29)

Which would you rather go through: physical pain or the pain of being completely abandoned by your friends? Which would be worse: extreme guilt or extreme shame? Would you rather be dressed in a silly outfit or stripped naked and paraded around in front of a multitude? Ideally, we'd avoid any and all of these kinds of suffering if we could. We'd choose carefully between them if we absolutely had to. But Jesus suffered them all.

Of all the people who have ever lived, Jesus was the least deserving of suffering. He never hurt anyone. He gave his time freely, even when he was exhausted. He had never done anything wrong, so he had no reason of his own to feel guilt or shame. However, as he was handed over to a company of Roman soldiers, they beat him mercilessly, releasing every bit of pent-up aggression they had been holding back. They mocked him for their own entertainment. Finally, they followed the orders handed down to them and nailed him to a cross along with two lawbreakers who had earned their own executions.

Little did those soldiers know, Jesus suffered for them. And those friends who vowed that they would never leave Jesus (and then left him)—Jesus suffered for them too. What about the rulers who felt so threatened by Jesus' popularity and influence? Jesus suffered for them too. The same goes for the criminals on either side, the people who had cried out to set a violent man free and send their Lord to the cross, the women who cried for him, and every passerby who wondered what the commotion was all about. Jesus suffered for all of them and for all of us, bearing our guilt and shame as he was nailed to a tree.

If we ever hurt in such a way—whether physically or emotionally—that it seems no one else could possibly understand what we are going through, we should remember what Jesus suffered. We have a God who took on flesh, lived in our world, and knows what it feels like to suffer. In his divine compassion, he suffered with us. The greater result, however, is that he suffered for us, and by doing so he won for us an eternal future free of all suffering: no guilt, no shame, no loneliness or ridicule, no pain of any kind ever again. Thank you, Jesus!

Prayer: Lord Jesus, when suffering comes into my life, help me bear up under it and look ahead to the joyous future you have earned for me. Amen.

E.D.S.

For further reading, see The People's Bible commentary on Matthew, pages 413-414.

Forsaken

Bible Reading: Matthew 27:45-50

About three in the afternoon Jesus cried out in a loud voice, *"Eli, Eli, lema sabachthani?"* (which means "My God, my God, why have you forsaken me?"). (Matthew 27:46)

One of the worst feelings a human being can know is that of loneliness. And sociologists say that emotion is becoming almost epidemic. Even as technology affords new ways of staying connected with others, many seem to be losing the ability to make personal and fulfilling connections of friendship. Over time, a sense of loneliness affects an individual negatively, causing depression and anxiety, and it can even contribute to cardiovascular disease and other health risks. Whether it affects our health or not, loneliness never feels good, especially when that loneliness darkens our hearts as we are thronged by people.

As Jesus hung on the cross, there was no shortage of people around him. Many considered him their enemy; a few knew him as their teacher and friend; one heartbroken woman called him her son. Not many people would look at this scene and say he was alone. Still, while darkness covered the land in the middle of the day, he was lonely—and it wasn't just a feeling. Jesus experienced the reality of God's judgment in a tangible way. He was forsaken by God.

Throughout human history, plenty of people have tried to run and hide from God: Adam and Eve, Cain, and Jonah may come to mind, but they weren't the only ones. Each one of them found, however, that if God is looking for you, he will find you; there is nowhere on earth we can go that he is not. God is present everywhere in all of creation, especially with his people—everywhere, that is, except hell. Though God has complete dominion over hell, all who reside there will only ever know the absence of God's presence and the withholding of all his blessing, which is a result of his absolute authority and his righteous judgment for those who reject him in stubborn unbelief. Hell is a God-forsaken place, and there the suffering is immeasurable and eternal.

This is what Jesus experienced as he neared death on the cross—and it was the direct result of our sin. As our substitute, Jesus bore our God-forsaken guilt when the Father abandoned his perfect Son. All of God's wrath was focused on Jesus so that every sinner in the world could be reconciled to God. In that moment Jesus truly became the Lamb of God who takes away the sin of the world. Now we can be sure that even though we may experience feelings of loneliness at times, for Jesus' sake, our God will never leave us alone.

Prayer: Jesus, thank you for satisfying God's righteous wrath for me. Help me remember that you will never leave me or forsake me. Amen.

E.D.S.

For further reading, see The People's Bible commentary on Matthew, pages 418-423.

The Curtain Is Torn

Bible Reading: Matthew 27:51-56

At that moment the curtain of the temple was torn in two from top to bottom. (Matthew 27:51)

How many books or movies can you think of that are centered on some form of treasure hunting? It makes for a great story when a character is after something extremely valuable—maybe even priceless—but must find a way to get to it. The target may be a pile of money in a highly secured vault, a historical artifact tucked away in a booby-trapped cave, or a famous work of art heavily guarded in a museum. Those of us who enjoy such stories watch and wait as the main characters devise a plan and then work their way through or around the obstacles to gain access to the treasure.

What every human being ought to be concerned about isn't a made-up story, though. As we face eternity, we all need to find a way to gain access to God's holy presence. This is no small task for sinful people. Any plans we may devise will never be able to penetrate the great barrier that our sin and guilt have erected between our corrupted souls and the righteous Lord. Even if, by some chance, we could find a way in, we would never survive the experience, since God's holiness does not permit him to tolerate even the slightest bit of evil—and we are entirely covered in impurity from birth.

The temple curtain served as a constant reminder of the people's inability to stroll into God's presence; no sinner could survive an attempt to breach the barrier into the Most Holy Place. The only access was through a high priest who sprinkled the blood of an innocent sacrifice, and even he could enter only once a year. However, when Jesus, our Great High Priest, offered himself on the cross as a once-for-all sacrifice for sinners, his holy blood gained access for us to the very presence of God—not merely a room in a temple but the glorious eternal home of God, his angels, and all whom he graciously invites to join him. The curtain was torn from top to bottom as God accepted his Son's offering—the full payment that removed our sin and guilt. Jesus' spotless life given in place of ours satisfied God's wrath and justice forever.

Through faith in Jesus, we have access to God. One day he will welcome us to the feast he has prepared; until then we pray in Jesus' name, knowing that for his sake the Father hears and answers according to his good plans for us. No treasure in this life can measure up to the lasting goodness of God's presence. Through Jesus' life and death for us, we have open access to enter and rejoice in God's presence forever.

Prayer: Jesus, only through you do I have access to the Father. Fill me with joy in your eternal presence. Amen.

E.D.S.

For further reading, see The People's Bible commentary on Matthew, pages 424-430.

The Greatest Escape

Bible Reading: Matthew 27:62-66

"Take a guard," Pilate answered. "Go, make the tomb as secure as you know how." 66 So they went and made the tomb secure by putting a seal on the stone and posting the guard. (Matthew 27:65-66)

In 1933, the United States federal government took over an island near San Francisco and turned it into a prison for some of the most dangerous prisoners: bank robbers, murderers, and gangsters—the kind of people who caused trouble at other prisons and needed extra layers of security. Alcatraz Island was the ideal place to keep such violent criminals because strong currents and cold water temperatures meant that even if anyone escaped, he likely wouldn't survive a swim toward land. Attempts were made, but of the 36 men who tried to escape, all were either apprehended on the island, killed during their escape attempts, or are presumed to have drowned.

How much security does a dead man need? Apart from a few miracles worked at the hands of some prophets and Jesus himself, dead people didn't generally come back to life. Even those who had been raised for a time ultimately died again, proving that death comes to us all without exception and without escape. Still, Jesus' enemies argued for a guard at his tomb. If this dead man's followers even made claims of a resurrection, Jesus would remain a problem that wouldn't die even though his body did. So they arranged for a guard to be posted and a seal to be placed on the tomb.

On the third day, however, all these precautions wound up serving as even greater proof of Jesus' power over the grave. The guards witnessed an earthquake and saw an angel open the tomb. The body they had been guarding was nowhere to be seen. The seal hadn't been broken until the angel moved the stone away, proving that no one had tampered with the grave from the outside; no, the one *inside* the tomb had freed himself by the power of God!

Jesus was the first dead man to rise from the grave in glory and exaltation, but he will not be the last. All who hoped in him and left their bodies behind when they died can be sure that their bodies too will be raised to live forever in glory. All who trust in Jesus can be confident that death is now a temporary state that will be undone forever when he returns. Temporary also are the pain, grief, and loss that come when a brother or sister in Christ leaves this world for the next. No enemy of ours can secure our graves to prevent our escape—Jesus is and always will be undefeated by death.

Prayer: Jesus, thank you for the sure hope that is mine through your resurrection from the grave. As long as I have time, help me share this hope with others. Amen.

E.D.S.

For further reading, see The People's Bible commentary on Matthew, pages 432-434.

Don't Be Surprised

Bible Reading: Matthew 28:1-10

"He is not here; he has risen, just as he said. Come and see the place where he lay." (Matthew 28:6)

At certain times in our lives, we might be blessed beyond our expectations. Perhaps we face a situation with our nerves on edge, cautiously optimistic that things could work out. We pray and carry out our tasks to the best of the abilities God has given us, and the successful outcome exceeds what we thought was even possible. Perhaps we have asked for God's watchful care on behalf of a loved one going in for a risky surgery and are greeted with the doctor's announcement that everything went even better than they had hoped. But we've likely had times too when it seemed as if our plans had completely failed and everything was falling apart. Only in hindsight do we realize that the circumstances were leading us down a different path and were presenting us with an entirely different opportunity, one we hadn't even considered as an option. We shouldn't be surprised. God has promised to give good things to his children—and he does, just as he said he would.

As the women made their way to the tomb of their Lord on Easter morning, what were they expecting? Surely they expected to see the same body exactly where they had seen Joseph place it late on Friday afternoon. They planned to honor their teacher and friend by wrapping his lifeless remains in spices, as was their burial custom—a custom that had been delayed in observance of the Sabbath Day laws. As they went to the tomb, perhaps they were praying for strength, peace, and comfort in their loss—anything that would give them hope for the days ahead. God gave them blessings far beyond what they expected.

The angel announced that the women wouldn't be finding a body—it wasn't there anymore. Why not? "He has risen, just as he said." That shouldn't have surprised them, because Sunday morning marked the third day—the day Jesus had promised he would return to life. This same Jesus had also foretold that he would fulfill every prophecy, would give rest to all who'd come to him weary and burdened, and would be crucified to take away the sins of the world. No one should have been surprised; it all happened just as Jesus had said.

Jesus also promised that he will come again in glory. Because he kept every other pledge to us and fulfilled his Word, we need not fear the final judgment. Instead, we look forward with anticipation that he will bring eternal blessings far beyond anything we can imagine. We know that our sins are paid for and forgiven, his righteousness is ours through the faith we've been given, and we'll soon see him face-to-face—just as he said.

Prayer: Lord Jesus, thank you for fulfilling your mission and fulfilling your promises. Your resurrection gives me a living hope. Amen.

E.D.S.

For further reading, see The People's Bible commentary on Matthew, pages 434-439.

The Right Tools

Bible Reading: Matthew 28:16-20

"Therefore go and make disciples of all nations, baptizing them in the name of the Father and of the Son and of the Holy Spirit, [20] and teaching them to obey everything I have commanded you. And surely I am with you always, to the very end of the age." (Matthew 28:19-20)

If you've ever tried to pound a nail with a wrench or attempted to use a butter knife to cut a steak, you know how important it is to have the right tool for the job. An inadequate substitute results in frustration, futility, and even the possibility of injury. A master woodworker may have an entire wall filled with files, clamps, bits, and saw blades because different materials and different cuts can call for specialized tools made for specialized tasks. A mechanic probably has drawers of wrenches and sockets. To work on the various parts of a wide range of vehicles, he or she needs to be able to tighten or loosen a wide range of nuts and bolts. The right tools make all the difference.

What tools do disciples need? How do we fight against evil and unbelief in a corrupt and defiled world? How do we grow in our own faith and rescue the lost who are living in darkness? How many tools do we need to give comfort to the grieving, hope to the helpless, forgiveness to the guilt-stricken, and sight to the spiritually blind? How many tools must it take to relate to people of widely differing backgrounds, cultures, ages, and education levels?

Jesus gives us two tools: Word and sacrament. No doubt the almighty God can create or strengthen faith through any means he chooses. However, he has bound himself to these means of grace and has assured us that we can expect his Word to accomplish what he desires every time we speak it, read it, learn it, and study it. Baptism is a onetime gift that brings eternal blessings to young and old as the Holy Spirit plants and nurtures faith and marks the baptized as God's own children. The Lord's Supper unites believers in faith and forgives sins as we eat and drink the very body and blood of Christ in, with, and under the bread and wine. Jesus' disciples of every generation can be fully confident that in these tools we have all we need to build and strengthen the church until he comes again.

Jesus is always with us. Yet he promises an extra measure of his presence as we grow together through Word and sacrament. With Word and sacrament, we encourage one another. With Word and sacrament, we invite others to join us in following the one who lived, died, rose, and ascended as our eternal Savior. May we always faithfully use the tools he has given us to do his work!

Prayer: Jesus, thank you for your saving work and for equipping us as your disciples. Bless our efforts to reach others with your saving name. Amen.

E.D.S.

For further reading, see The People's Bible commentary on Matthew, pages 440-444.

Get Ready for Jesus

Bible Reading: Mark 1:1-8

As it is written in Isaiah the prophet: "I will send my messenger ahead of you, who will prepare your way." (Mark 1:2)

And so John the Baptist appeared in the wilderness, preaching a baptism of repentance for the forgiveness of sins. (Mark 1:4)

If you were preparing for a job interview, you would do whatever you could to make yourself look good. Put on your best clothes. Recall your achievements. Highlight your best qualities. The goal is to make yourself look impressive. You want to earn a job.

John the Baptist prepared people for an important meeting—a meeting with Jesus. His instructions for preparing to meet Jesus did not include making yourself look good. In fact, John said to highlight the bad. He preached a baptism of repentance. Repentance includes confessing your sinfulness. It means admitting that you are not worthy to be in God's presence because of who you are and what you do. This is the attitude that makes people ready for Jesus.

Isn't this an odd way to prepare to meet someone important? Typically you want others to think you are worthy of them and their attention. You hide the bad and pretend you're good. You clean up even if you're usually dirty; you act confident even if you're not; you try to impress even if you think you're unimpressive.

But the preparation John preached was different because of who the people were getting ready to meet. Jesus is the Son of God, the Lord, and the Savior. If Jesus were only the Son of God, you would want to hide your sins from him so he wouldn't punish you. If he were only the Lord, you would want to impress him so that he would find you worthy of his attention. But Jesus is also the Savior. He did not come to congratulate people on how good they have been. He is the Savior of sinners, and so we prepare to meet him with repentance.

John preached a baptism of repentance *for the forgiveness of sins*. Therefore, when you prepare to meet Jesus in his Word and in the sacraments, you hold up your sins to him. You are honest about your failures to live and think according to God's will. He comes to you to take those sins to the cross and to announce his forgiveness to you. Repent! Let the Word of God work sorrow over your sins. Then cling to the promise of your baptism—a washing that brings that forgiveness to you.

Prayer: Lord Jesus, work in me a genuine sorrow for my sinfulness. Thank you for saving sinners like me. Help me trust you alone as the reason I can stand before God. Amen.

A.J.D.

For further reading, see The People's Bible commentary on Mark, pages 9-15.

Attended by Angels

Bible Reading: Mark 1:12-13

He was in the wilderness forty days, being tempted by Satan. He was with the wild animals, and angels attended him. (Mark 1:13)

Did you notice that angels attended Jesus? But did you notice what they didn't do? They didn't stop the temptations from happening, and they didn't prevent his struggle. They knew Jesus was facing temptation for you. His struggle against temptation served an important purpose. He overcame the devil's temptation and avoided sin, and he gave you credit for his perfection. Jesus' struggle against temptation was part of winning salvation for you. He was your substitute in life. He was perfect in your place. And the angels didn't want to get in the way of that, so they didn't stop the struggle.

This wasn't the only time angels attended Jesus. They also strengthened him in the Garden of Gethsemane, hours before his death. But do you know what they didn't do? They didn't stop the crucifixion. They knew Jesus was suffering and dying for you. His suffering served a very important purpose. He received the punishment for sin, setting you free from that punishment. He was your substitute in death. He died in your place. And the angels didn't want to get in the way of that, so they didn't stop the crucifixion.

God has said that he sends his angels to serve you (see Psalm 91:11 and Hebrews 1:14). But do you know what they don't do? They don't stop every pain, every struggle, or every sadness. Why not?

Your pains, struggles, and sadnesses do not accomplish your salvation. Jesus has already done that for you. But those trials may serve for your good, or they may serve for the good of others who are encouraged in their struggles as they see you going through yours. Some struggles serve an important purpose that only your Father in heaven can see. If that is the case, angels will not stop them from happening. But the angels will attend you.

Jesus was not alone when he struggled in the wilderness or when he suffered in Gethsemane. Neither are you alone. Jesus is with you and knows what it's like to struggle. Your heavenly Father sees you and knows what you need. And "he will command his angels concerning you to guard you in all your ways" (Psalm 91:11). You do not go through your struggles alone!

Prayer: Heavenly Father, into your hands I commend my body and soul and all things. Let your holy angel be with me that the wicked foe may have no power over me. Amen.

A.J.D.

For further reading, see The People's Bible commentary on Mark, pages 18-19.

The Call to Ministry

Bible Reading: Mark 1:14-20

"Come, follow me," Jesus said, "and I will send you out to fish for people." [18] At once they left their nets and followed him. (Mark 1:17-18)

How foolish they were! Simon Peter, Andrew, James, and John left their nets and followed Jesus. They each left behind a good job and a safe means of income and followed the One who couldn't promise any earthly wealth.

How wonderful that they did! Not one of us would be benefiting from their fishing business today had they continued it, even if they had become millionaires. They wouldn't be enjoying their earnings anymore either. But we have benefited from their work of fishing for people. They too are still enjoying the results of their work as they daily see people join the ranks of the saints triumphant in heaven because of the message they preached.

Today, Jesus still provides fishers of people by calling men into the pastoral ministry. Tragically, young adults who are considering the ministry often hear loud voices discouraging them. Those voices say, "Think of all the things you could do and all the money you could make! What a waste it would be if you became a pastor!"

If you are inclined to steer a talented young man away from ministry, first consider this: Are the benefits of another career actually greater than the impact of ministry? Is it a waste for a young man to use his gifts to bring people to eternal life? Isn't this work important enough that we should encourage all those who have the gifts for it, even if their gifts could also serve well elsewhere? Seek out young people who are intelligent, talented, and personable. Encourage them to consider ministry. Be honest about the sacrifices, but also be honest about the importance of the work. They leave behind other opportunities and perhaps the potential to make more money, but they are doing work that affects eternal life and death! They preach the good news and catch people for God's kingdom, bringing to them God's law and gospel and preserving them for life with Jesus in eternity. Their talents are not wasted! They are put to noble use!

It is true that ministry is not the only God-pleasing way to use the gifts God has given. But no one in heaven will regret being a pastor, even if he was not rich and famous on earth. He will see the people who benefited from his preaching and teaching of God's Word, people who will say, "Thank you for being my pastor. You gave me what was most important." And he will join us as we praise and thank Jesus for calling people into ministry for our eternal benefit.

Prayer: Lord Jesus, call many more to be fishers of people, that we may benefit eternally from their work. Amen.

A.J.D.

For further reading, see The People's Bible commentary on Mark, pages 20-23.

Jesus Versus the Demon

Bible Reading: Mark 1:21-28

Just then a man in their synagogue who was possessed by an impure spirit cried out, [24] "What do you want with us, Jesus of Nazareth? Have you come to destroy us? I know who you are—the Holy One of God!"

[25] "Be quiet!" said Jesus sternly. "Come out of him!" [26] The impure spirit shook the man violently and came out of him with a shriek. (Mark 1:23-26)

There was a demon in church. Does that seem odd? Doesn't that seem like the last place a demon would be? This impure spirit possessed a man and was sitting through the synagogue service. The demon was quiet, until it witnessed the thing that it hated most: people listening to the Word of God.

This was the moment the demon made a scene, because the goal of Satan and the demons is to separate you from God. Their goal is not to cause you physical pain or make you poor. If a successful and satisfying life means you will see no need for a God and Savior, then they will be happy to allow such a life. If good health has given you no reason to cry out to God for help, they won't provide a reason for you to start. They want to keep you away from the Word of God and the name of Jesus. Yes, demons may be in churches to provide distractions and to keep you from taking the gospel to heart. They may also be behind the subtle, daily temptations that divert you from God's Word—whatever it takes to separate you from God!

Recognize the real danger of the spiritual forces of the dark world. The most serious danger is separation from God and the means of grace. Then, recognize the power that Jesus and his Word have over demons. When Jesus commanded the impure spirit to be quiet and come out of the man, it had to obey. It had no choice! Jesus' Word has authority over demons!

The preaching of the Word may not sound powerful. But look at the effect it has! Demons cannot stand it! This is your confidence, child of God. You are marked with the name of Christ. It was placed on you at your baptism. You have the words of Jesus. Continue to listen to them. "Though devils all the world should fill, all eager to devour us, we tremble not, we fear no ill; they shall not overpow'r us" (CW 863:3)—because they cannot overpower Jesus.

Prayer: "Keep me as the apple of your eye; hide me in the shadow of your wings from the wicked who are out to destroy me, from my mortal enemies who surround me" (Psalm 17:8-9). Amen.

A.J.D.

For further reading, see The People's Bible commentary on Mark, pages 24-26.

Go See Jesus, Then Go Serve

Bible Reading: Mark 1:29-34

Simon's mother-in-law was in bed with a fever, and they immediately told Jesus about her.
31 So he went to her, took her hand and helped her up. The fever left her and she began to wait on them.
32 That evening after sunset the people brought to Jesus all the sick and demon-possessed.
33 The whole town gathered at the door. (Mark 1:30-33)

The whole town gathered at the door! What brought them there? Surely, it was Jesus, but there was something else that brought them to his doorstep—they had problems. If there had been no illnesses or problems in Capernaum, there would have been fewer one-on-one encounters with Jesus. Jesus gave his attention to each person who came to him. He turned no one away, even though it had been a long day for him.

No one wants to struggle through life. No one looks forward to strained relationships, health complications, career failures, or emotional pain. These result from sin. They are not good things. But Jesus can use them for good when he uses them to bring you to him. These problems may drive you to Jesus' doorstep because you have found nowhere else to go with them. Whether you consider yourself important or not, whether you consider your problems to be big or not, Jesus gives you his attention.

The problems caused the people to go see Jesus. Then what? After Jesus healed Simon's mother-in-law, she responded by doing what she had been doing before she became ill. She began to wait on them. The gift of health wasn't only for her own benefit. Jesus' gift gave her the opportunity to serve others.

Life's troubles drive you to go see Jesus. Then his gifts provide you the opportunity to go serve others. What is he encouraging you to do today? Make a quick inventory of your life. List the blessings, the things that are going well, the gifts and the abilities you have. Also list the challenges, the struggles, the temptations, the problems. If the challenges today outweigh the gifts, perhaps he is encouraging you to spend more one-on-one time with him. Continue to meditate on his Word. Receive the Lord's Supper. Wrestle with him in prayer. If the gifts today outweigh the challenges, perhaps he is encouraging you to turn your attention to others. How may you serve today? Give your attention to the needs of others, and use your gifts for their benefit.

Go see Jesus. Then go serve.

Prayer: Jesus, use the challenges in my life to bring me closer to you. Help me see opportunities to serve others with the gifts you have given me. Amen.

A.J.D.

For further reading, see The People's Bible commentary on Mark, pages 26-28.

A Break for Prayer

Bible Reading: Mark 1:35-39

Very early in the morning, while it was still dark, Jesus got up, left the house and went off to a solitary place, where he prayed. (Mark 1:35)

Someone might suggest that Jesus didn't have time to pray. It had been a busy Sabbath Day. He preached in the synagogue, and he drove out a demon there. After the synagogue service, Jesus went to the home of Simon Peter and Andrew. Instead of finding a place for a nap, Jesus found Simon's mother-in-law in bed with a fever. He went to her and healed her. That night Jesus' popularity prevented him from enjoying a well-deserved early bedtime, as the whole town gathered at the door after the sun went down. Jesus gave time to each person. With a busy day, a late night, and plans to travel the next day to preach somewhere else, it seems he didn't have time to pray.

Yet Jesus made time to pray. He didn't create an extra hour in the day just for himself. He made time by making prayer a top priority. After a busy day and a late night, he got up early in the morning to pray and went to a solitary place with no distractions. Being with people—preaching to them and helping them—was clearly important. Talking to his heavenly Father was just as important. He had to do it, even if it meant choosing prayer over something else. If prayer is that important to Jesus, the perfect Son of God, who are we to claim that prayer isn't necessary or important for us?

We might be busy too. Our lives are time-bound, and we often run out of time to do everything we want to do. But when we say we don't have time to pray, the truth is that we are choosing to do something else with our time. We choose to work, serve, eat, study, work out, and sleep. We choose to clean, talk, play, and run errands. These are all important things, and they all take time, but it's a lie of the sinful nature to claim that we have no time to pray.

Colossians 4:2 says, "Devote yourselves to prayer." Jesus had many things on his mind and on his calendar, and he considered prayer to be essential and beneficial for a busy schedule. Trust Jesus on that. Entrust to your heavenly Father all the things on your mind and on your calendar. Make prayer a priority, and discover the benefits your Father intends for your life of prayer.

Prayer: Heavenly Father, help me find time and places to pray to you regularly. Bless my life of prayer. Amen.

A.J.D.

For further reading, see The People's Bible commentary on Mark, pages 28-30.

Jesus Knows Better

Bible Reading: Mark 1:40-45

Jesus sent him away at once with a strong warning: 44 "See that you don't tell this to anyone. . . . " 45 Instead he went out and began to talk freely, spreading the news. As a result, Jesus could no longer enter a town openly but stayed outside in lonely places. (Mark 1:43-45)

Jesus healed a man with leprosy. When Jesus told him not to tell anyone what had happened, the man instead "went out and began to talk freely." Why did he do that? He probably had a good reason. Ever since Adam blamed Eve for eating the fruit in the Garden of Eden, people have been good at convincing themselves that they have good reasons to disobey God. Whatever the reason was, however, the man disobeyed. "As a result, Jesus could no longer enter a town openly but stayed outside in lonely places." You see, Jesus had a reason for the command he had given the man even if the man didn't understand what that reason was. Jesus knew better.

Do you know better than Jesus? You probably would never say that you do. But your actions sometimes communicate that. Jesus has a reason for the commands he gives us. However, you might still lash out in anger, thinking that you are justified in doing so. You might still cultivate lust in your mind, assuming that it doesn't hurt anyone to only think about it. You might still try to serve both God and money, thinking that you can balance the two better than most. We are great at convincing ourselves that our reasons for disobeying are good enough. But disobedience is disobedience, even when you think your actions are justified. Jesus knows better!

Your disobedience, however, does not stop Jesus from loving you. Jesus wanted to heal this man, even though the man would misuse that gift. Jesus was willing to take the man's place outside the city and give the man his place inside the city. That's God's grace. He continues to give you good gifts even when he knows that you might misuse them. He even was willing to take your place under the punishment for sin and give you his place as child of God.

Jesus does know better, so cling to his Word. You can do it! He gives you gifts, and he gives you commands. Remember that he gives both to benefit you. He gives both because he knows what is best.

Prayer: Jesus, thank you for the gifts you graciously give me every day. Help me use them properly, and forgive me when I don't. Thank you for the commands you have given. Help me trust them and obey them. Amen.

A.J.D.

For further reading, see The People's Bible commentary on Mark, pages 30-33.

Jesus Gives More Than You Ask For

Bible Reading: Mark 2:1-12

When Jesus saw their faith, he said to the paralyzed man, "Son, your sins are forgiven." (Mark 2:5)

10 **"I want you to know that the Son of Man has authority on earth to forgive sins." So he said to the man,** 11 **"I tell you, get up, take your mat and go home."** (Mark 2:10-11)

The man came to be healed. That's why his friends went through so much trouble. They carried him to the house where Jesus was, tried to get in the door, then dug through the clay and branches and dirt that made up the roof to lower him down through the hole. They did it! They got him in! The paralyzed man could finally see Jesus.

The paralyzed man came to be healed. So how do you think he reacted when Jesus said, "Son, your sins are forgiven"? Did his heart sink in disappointment? Did he roll his eyes and think, "Enough with this spiritual talk! I have a real problem here"? Or maybe, for the first time in a long time, the man breathed a sigh of relief.

Jesus didn't always announce forgiveness before he did a miracle, but he knew something about this man. Jesus knew this was exactly what he needed. Had this man's conscience been giving him as much trouble as his paralysis had? Jesus knew that this man's newly healthy body wouldn't be whole with a guilty conscience. So first he gave the man what he needed most—a clean conscience, peace, a new life—even before he could walk. The man had come to be healed. Jesus gave so much more.

Jesus knows exactly what you need, and he often gives more or better than what you ask for. A sermon or a devotion occasionally seems as if it were written just for you and your specific situation. An unexpected and even unwanted answer to a prayer turns out to be something better than you could have foreseen. In every case, Jesus knows exactly what you need. He may not give you exactly what you ask for, but he does want you to breathe a sigh of relief. He says to you, "I forgive you all your sins." Then he answers your prayers in a way that's right for you.

Go to Jesus with your problems. Ask him for help, for solutions. Listen to him speak to you in his Word. Keep spending time with Jesus and see if he doesn't give you even more and better than you ask for.

Prayer: Jesus, in your grace, give me what you know I need. Amen.

A.J.D.

For further reading, see The People's Bible commentary on Mark, pages 33-37.

Jesus Has the Authority to Forgive Your Sins

Bible Reading: Mark 2:1-12

"I want you to know that the Son of Man has authority on earth to forgive sins." So he said to the man, [11] "I tell you, get up, take your mat and go home." [12] He got up, took his mat and walked out in full view of them all. (Mark 2:10-12)

A boy was meticulously building a tower with his blocks. He was proud of his creation. Then, his sister carelessly ran through the room, knocking the whole construction to the ground. In his anger, the boy yelled after her, "You go to your room and stay there! You're grounded!"

The girl called over her shoulder, "You can't tell me what to do. You're not Mom or Dad." She was right. He didn't have the authority to hand out or enforce a punishment.

That was the objection of the teachers of the law. Jesus had said, "Son, your sins are forgiven." But they were sure Jesus didn't have the authority to forgive sins. Forgiveness of sins means that God does not hold those sins against the person who is guilty of them. Therefore, only God can make that pronouncement. Only God can actually forgive sins.

The teachers of the law were right about that, but they were wrong about Jesus. Jesus is God, which means he can forgive sins. But how do you prove that sins are forgiven? Forgiveness can't be seen. So Jesus did something that can be seen. He did something that, like forgiveness, only God can do: He made a paralytic walk. The miracle proved that he is God and that he does have the authority to forgive sins.

Jesus has the authority to send your sins away "as far as the east is from the west" (Psalm 103:12). Forgiveness is not saying that sinfulness is not a big deal. Forgiveness is removing your sins and sending them away. God doesn't see them. They are no longer on your record. Jesus has the authority to do that. He doesn't say, "I hope your sins don't count against you" or "I think your sins are forgiven." He has the authority to make them gone because he is the one who paid their penalty with his death.

And then, with that authority, he has given us a wonderful privilege: "If you forgive anyone's sins, their sins are forgiven" (John 20:23). When your pastor or another Christian announces forgiveness to you, it is with Christ's authority. It is as if Jesus himself were telling you, "Your sins are forgiven!"

Prayer: Jesus, "wash away all my iniquity and cleanse me from my sin" (Psalm 51:2). Amen.

A.J.D.

For further reading, see The People's Bible commentary on Mark, pages 34-37.

It's for You

Bible Reading: Mark 2:23-28

Then he said to them, "The Sabbath was made for man, not man for the Sabbath. [28] So the Son of Man is Lord even of the Sabbath." (Mark 2:27-28)

Why do you go to church? Do you go for God, to praise and thank him? Do you go for your parents or spouse, to make them happy? Or is it for you?

Jesus had to correct the Pharisees. They were treating the Sabbath Day as something they did for God. The Sabbath Day was the seventh day of the week, Saturday. In the Old Testament, the Lord had told the Israelites to make this a day of rest—a day when they would not work but would gather for a sacred assembly. The Pharisees, however, added extra rules, thinking they would show how much they could do for God by how little they would do on the Sabbath.

Jesus said, "The Sabbath was made for man." God didn't benefit from the people resting; they did! God didn't benefit from the Sabbath assemblies; the people did! They received assurances that their sins were covered. In the same way, God doesn't benefit from you going to church; it's for you!

That's how God works. It's always for you. He created the world for people to use and enjoy, not people for the world. He became truly human, not for his own enjoyment but for you, so his perfect life could be presented to God as the substitute for yours. Jesus was crucified, died, and was buried, not for his own benefit but for you and for your salvation. Now he rules over all things at the right hand of God, not to satisfy his own desires but for you. God has done it all for you.

This is the God who wants you to get rest. He wants you to get physical rest. He doesn't require rest on Saturday, but he does want you to take breaks. Rest benefits you. He wants you to get spiritual rest also. He applies his perfect life and innocent death to you personally. He says, "I forgive you," so that you can rest knowing he will not punish you for your sins. He wants to address and remove the guilt from your past. He wants to inform you of his promises and build up your trust in those promises. He does these things through his Word and sacraments, which are found at church! That's why he wants you to go. You can thank and praise him there, but God isn't the one who benefits from your church attendance—it's for you!

Prayer: Lord, give me rest for my body and my soul. Amen.

A.J.D.

For further reading, see The People's Bible commentary on Mark, pages 43-45.

Demons Answer the Question

Bible Reading: Mark 3:7-12

Whenever the impure spirits saw him, they fell down before him and cried out, "You are the Son of God." (Mark 3:11)

The gospel of Mark aims to answer the question "Who is Jesus?" We give an answer to that question when we say the Apostles' Creed: "I believe in Jesus Christ, his only Son, our Lord." Jesus is the Son of God. We say it routinely. Often we say it while standing. Sometimes we say it while sitting. Almost every time we say it with no change in heart rate.

The demons here also gave an answer to that question. But consider how they said it. The impure spirits "fell down before him and cried out, 'You are the Son of God.'" That knowledge terrified them. They couldn't sit or stand when they said it—they fell down in front of him. They didn't recite the words without thinking about them; they shouted them in fear.

Demons reacted to Jesus with terror because they knew exactly who he was. They knew he had the power to destroy them. They knew his justice required him to destroy them because they had rebelled against God. They knew there was nothing they could do to stop that. Jesus is the Son of God—that is a terrifying truth for impure spirits.

What about for you? Jesus is the Son of God—is that good news or bad news for you? The Son of God knows your thoughts, your words, your actions. The Son of God has the power to judge and to destroy. Should you fall down in terror too? You have rebelled against him. Every sin is rebellion against God, because every sin is opposition to God's design for life. God is just. God is powerful. He must and can punish sin. Jesus is the Son of God. If even demons reacted to Jesus with terror, shouldn't you?

The demons knew who Jesus was. However, this truth brought them no comfort. Jesus wasn't born for them. He was born for you. The Son of God became human so that he could be your substitute. He uses his power and authority for you, not against you. He used that power to earn you entrance into God's favor with his perfect life. He used the authority to declare you not guilty after suffering the punishment for your sins. Jesus is the Son of God. Fall before him with reverence and rejoicing, not with terror. He is the Son of God! That's good news for you!

Prayer: Jesus, Son of God, thank you for using your power and authority for my benefit. Amen.

A.J.D.

For further reading, see The People's Bible commentary on Mark, pages 47-50.

The "Experts" Answer the Question

Bible Reading: Mark 3:20-30

When his family heard about this, they went to take charge of him, for they said, "He is out of his mind."

22 And the teachers of the law who came down from Jerusalem said, "He is possessed by Beelzebul! By the prince of demons he is driving out demons." (Mark 3:21-22)

"Who is Jesus?" It's the big question in Mark. Even demons knew the correct answer (Mark 3:11). However, it can be discouraging to hear the world's experts talk about Jesus. Throughout history many have claimed that Jesus was not really God. Some today think there is no place for Jesus in an enlightened society.

Some have even concluded that following all of Jesus' teachings is detrimental to societal progress. These opinions are discouraging because they come from people with influence. Others trust and follow. You may be left wondering if you're the crazy one for following Jesus.

The experts in the world have always had an opinion on the question "Who is Jesus?" The teachers of the law from the important city of Jerusalem accused Jesus of being possessed by Beelzebul, another name for the devil. These teachers were important people. They influenced others. How discouraging! But the teachers were not the only ones. Jesus' own family members had an opinion about him too. At this point in his life, they thought he was out of his mind.

The experts in the world, and maybe even members of your family, have opinions of Jesus that are quite different from yours. You are not the first to experience this! Don't be surprised, and don't get discouraged! We trust God more than we trust people, who have been wrong in the past and will be wrong again in the future. We trust the Word of God more than we trust our feelings and fears, which so easily change. God's Word endures forever. Jesus' Word was true when challenged by the experts of his day, it remains true when challenged by the experts of today, and it will continue to be true when challenged in the future.

One day, when Jesus returns, "every eye will see him" (Revelation 1:7) and "every tongue [will] acknowledge that Jesus Christ is Lord" (Philippians 2:11). On that day everyone will know that you were right to follow Jesus. You were right to trust his Word and hold on to his commands.

When Jesus faced hostile opinions, he answered them and carried on. There were more important things to do than to worry about what people think. Let's do the same. Be prepared to give an answer, but then get back to trusting

God's promises and loving your neighbor. His Word is not opinion—it is truth!

Prayer: Lord, give me courage to hold on to your Word no matter what others say or think. Amen.

A.J.D.

For further reading, see The People's Bible commentary on Mark, pages 55-58.

Jesus' Family

Bible Reading: Mark 3:31-35

> **Then he looked at those seated in a circle around him and said, "Here are my mother and my brothers!**
> **35 Whoever does God's will is my brother and sister and mother."** (Mark 3:34-35)

Family provides the closest relationships humans have. So when Jesus' mother and brothers came to see him, we may be a little surprised by what took place. To start with, it wasn't intended to be a pleasant visit. Jesus' mother and brothers had come to take charge of him because they thought he was out of his mind. When Jesus was told that they had arrived, he responded with a strange question: "Who are my mother and my brothers?" What a strange question! Was he disowning his own blood relatives?

No, not at all. Jesus' comment about family was not about them. It was about you. When someone mentioned family, Jesus took the opportunity to teach about family in God's kingdom. He was not putting his family down. He was lifting you up into that closest of relationships.

You see, not only Mary and her children get to be Jesus' family—you do too. Whoever does God's will is family to him.

Did your heart sink, though, when you read that? "Whoever does God's will." Who can do that? Multiple times within the past day you have failed to keep God's commands with pure thoughts and motives. But perfect obedience of the commandments is not what Jesus meant by doing God's will. He said in John 6:40, "My Father's will is that everyone who looks to the Son and believes in him shall have eternal life." God's will is that you trust that Jesus has provided your place in his kingdom with his life and death.

This means that not only the best of the best enjoy the closest of relationships with Jesus—*whoever* does God's will is Jesus' family. No one will hear the words "except you." *Any* individual who trusts that Jesus lived and died for him or her is family to Jesus. Nothing else about you comes into consideration. Your biological family, your history, your reputation or popularity, your level of involvement, your talents, the severity of your sins—these don't even come into consideration. He has covered your life with his. Jesus considers any individual who trusts his Word to be the closest of family. To him, nothing matters more than you.

Prayer: Jesus, thank you for making me part of your family. Help me trust your will in all things. Amen.

A.J.D.

For further reading, see The People's Bible commentary on Mark, pages 58-60.

His Word Has Power

Bible Reading: Mark 4:26-29

"Night and day, whether he sleeps or gets up, the seed sprouts and grows, though he does not know how." (Mark 4:27)

A child puts dirt in a cup and presses a bean into the dirt. She makes sure it has enough water and is in a sunny location. She will check on it occasionally and add water, but she has done all she can to turn this bean into a bean plant. Now it's up to the bean itself to sprout and grow. It's amazing. One day the child notices that a little green sprout has begun curling out of the bean and has pushed its way through the soil. How did that happen?

Jesus told a quick story about a man planting seeds. The man planted and cultivated, and then he went to bed. He was able to sleep because he knew he had done his part. He couldn't force the plants to grow. The seeds would sprout and grow on their own, even if he didn't completely understand how the process worked. The power to grow was in the seeds all along.

Jesus used this parable to describe the power of his Word. The power to cause growth is in the Word, not in the one planting the Word. We can plant it by reading Scripture for ourselves and by speaking it to others, but the power to grow and produce results is found in the message itself. The Word of God—the Bible—must remain the center of our lives and our worship for us to receive a lasting peace, a stronger faith, and a servant's heart.

If you sit and watch a plant carefully, you will not be able to see it growing. It is only when you come back later that you notice the growth which has taken place. It is the same with God's Word. You may not feel the Word working in you. It may seem as if nothing changes when you go to church or study God's Word. But Jesus says that the Word works. Don't give up on your devotions just because you don't notice a difference. Don't become discouraged with church or with reading God's Word just because you think it's not working. Most often the Word produces growth that can't be seen or felt immediately. It may not be until later that you notice how growth has taken place. But it will. You have Jesus' word on it.

Prayer: Lord God, bless my use of your Word. May it produce results in my life and in the lives of those with whom I share it. Amen.

A.J.D.

For further reading, see The People's Bible commentary on Mark, pages 65-66.

Power and Care

Bible Reading: Mark 4:35-41

Jesus was in the stern, sleeping on a cushion. The disciples woke him and said to him, "Teacher, don't you care if we drown?"
39 He got up, rebuked the wind and said to the waves, "Quiet! Be still!" Then the wind died down and it was completely calm.
40 He said to his disciples, "Why are you so afraid? Do you still have no faith?" (Mark 4:38-40)

Jesus has power over nature. Even though people have made many great advances throughout history, we still cannot control the weather. We can predict it. We can prepare for it. But we can't control it. Jesus can. He spoke to the weather, and the weather obeyed him! Notice, though, that Jesus didn't prevent the storm from happening. While the storm was raging, Jesus did nothing about it. In fact, he was sleeping! The disciples knew

Jesus had the power to stop the storm, but he hadn't yet. That led them to a frightening conclusion: Maybe Jesus doesn't care.

Have you ever wondered if God cares? Have your eyes or your feelings convinced you that God must not care? If he has power over nature, he certainly has power over things that happen in your life. So when something goes wrong, why doesn't God stop it from happening? Why doesn't he use his power to take it away? Doesn't God care?

There's a false assumption behind that question. It's the assumption that a caring God equals an easy life for me. If God really cares about me, shouldn't he do everything the way I want him to? No, he shouldn't. Sometimes what you don't want turns out to be better for you in the long run. Jesus knows that. He can use even a storm to benefit you.

Jesus answered the false assumption of the disciples by asking, "Why are you so afraid? Do you still have no faith?" In other words, Jesus was asking why they thought this storm meant he didn't care. His promises were not going to fail just because there was a bad storm. The storm was not evidence that Jesus didn't care. It was evidence that sometimes scary things happen. But when scary things are in the hands of Jesus, they are not as scary because he has control. He will keep his promises to you. He will do what is best for you because he wants to and because he can.

Jesus has power, and Jesus cares. Both are true. You are in good hands.

Prayer: Jesus, be with me through the moments I can't control. Use your power to care for me. Amen.

A.J.D.

For further reading, see The People's Bible commentary on Mark, pages 68-71.

We Should Fear and Love Jesus

Bible Reading: Mark 5:1-20

When he saw Jesus from a distance, he ran and fell on his knees in front of him. [7] **He shouted at the top of his voice, "What do you want with me, Jesus, Son of the Most High God? In God's name don't torture me!"** (Mark 5:6-7)

And he begged Jesus again and again not to send them out of the area. (Mark 5:10)

What a terrifying experience! Can you imagine meeting a man with superhuman strength who lived in a cemetery? Can you imagine hearing his agonized voice and coming face-to-face with the legion of demons that possessed him? Just reading about it and thinking about it (especially while alone at night) can give you chills!

We may react to the thought of spirits and demons with terror. But have you noticed how the demons always reacted to Jesus? A powerful army of demons fell down before Jesus, shouting and begging him not to hurt them. If I am scared of demons and demons have an even greater fear of Jesus, then what should my attitude toward Jesus be?

We can be quick to listen to anyone who acts like an expert, but then we hesitate to trust what's in the Bible. We balk at calling something a sin when Jesus says it is just because the world doesn't want to call it sin. We resist following a commandment from Scripture because that would make us different from all the people around us who break it regularly. We make Scripture's main messages of law and gospel secondary because the world says there are other causes we should dedicate ourselves to. When we do this, we fear and respect the world's opinion. How cowardly we can be! Look at how the demons viewed Jesus.

Shouldn't we give Jesus and his Word the same kind of fear and respect that the demons showed?

Jesus is the one with authority over demons. He is the one who turned the demon-possessed man's life around. He can do that for you too by providing an anchor of truth and changelessness. Jesus is the one with compassion, who didn't come to seek and to save the pious and holy but to seek and to save the lost, the troubled, the wanderers, even the demon-possessed. He has truth for you. He has commandments for you that protect his blessings to you. He gives the peace of sins forgiven, the assurance of God's favor, and the promise of his providence until he takes you to eternal life with him. We should fear and love Jesus. He is worth listening to.

Prayer: Jesus, be my anchor. Help me trust your truth, and give my life a measure of peace. Amen.

A.J.D.

For further reading, see The People's Bible commentary on Mark, pages 72-75.

Jesus Gives Your Life Purpose

Bible Reading: Mark 5:1-20

As Jesus was getting into the boat, the man who had been demon-possessed begged to go with him.
19 Jesus did not let him, but said, "Go home to your own people and tell them how much the Lord has done for you, and how he has had mercy on you." (Mark 5:18-19)

Many people struggle with a lack of contentment. Wouldn't it be nice to live somewhere else or have a different job? Won't it be nice when I'm out of school . . . when I have a family . . . when the kids are a little older . . . when I can retire? It's not wrong to have goals or plans, but it can be wrong to be so focused on the "what ifs" and "should haves" that we fail to see the present as a situation God has placed in front of us.

Jesus had just driven demons from a man. After receiving such a gift, the man imagined the possibilities: Wouldn't it be great to leave this little town and to follow Jesus to important places, doing important things? His life would finally have meaning!

But Jesus didn't let him. There were people to impact right where he was. The man didn't have to travel far or do something different to be important. Jesus wanted him right there, telling people what had happened to him and what role Jesus had in it. Jesus gave the man's everyday life dignity by giving him purpose. The man would have an impact on real people, and it would mean everything to them.

God has blessed you with abilities specific to you. He has made you valuable and important by purchasing you with the blood of his Son and presenting you as blameless through Jesus' life and death. He has forgiven your past. Now he has important things for you to do today, in your current situation. He has given you purpose: to love and serve the specific people you encounter today. You may have opportunities to do different things in the future, but this is where Jesus wants you today. There are very real people around you today, people he cares for, people he wants to bless with a friend, a parent, an empathetic coworker, or a kind classmate by giving them you. Open your eyes and see your situation. Rejoice that God has given you opportunities to have an impact right where you are.

Prayer: Jesus, give me contentment in my daily life. Help me carry out the roles you have placed before me today. Amen.

A.J.D.

For further reading, see The People's Bible commentary on Mark, pages 72-75.

Jesus Has Time for You

Bible Reading: Mark 5:21-43

Then the woman, knowing what had happened to her, came and fell at his feet and, trembling with fear, told him the whole truth. [34] He said to her, "Daughter, your faith has healed you. Go in peace and be freed from your suffering."

[35] While Jesus was still speaking, some people came from the house of Jairus, the synagogue leader. "Your daughter is dead," they said. "Why bother the teacher anymore?" [36] Overhearing what they said, Jesus told him, "Don't be afraid; just believe." (Mark 5:33-36)

Jairus was a synagogue leader. He was important. Plus, he had an important problem. His little daughter was dying. Jesus went with him, and so did a large crowd. It was an important parade with important people on an important, urgent mission.

Then Jesus delayed the urgent mission to ask who touched him. A woman with a bleeding disease had touched him and was immediately healed. Jesus knew that. He could have kept walking, but he knew something about the woman. She had spent the last 12 years with struggle, frustration, embarrassment, and financial hardship. She was used to being in the shadows. That was how she viewed herself—an unimportant outcast. She wanted to slip in and out unnoticed, but Jesus wanted more and better for her. He stopped, gave her one-on-one time, and listened as she told him everything. She was already healed, but Jesus gave her even more. He gave her his full attention. He gave her warmth as he addressed her as "daughter." He showed her how important she was to him.

But what was Jairus feeling during this time? "Jesus, why are you stopping? To talk to an insignificant woman? This is important! My daughter! Life or death! Come on!" Did Jesus forget about Jairus? Of course not. So why did Jesus make him wait? Perhaps because he knew exactly what was best for Jairus. Jesus taught him patience, a lesson in God's timing and power.

You may wonder why God doesn't treat you the way he treats someone else. Perhaps it's because God is dealing with you as an individual. He doesn't treat you like anyone else because you are not anyone else. He may make you wait. He may help you right away. He may give you what you ask for. He may do something different. He may allow you to struggle. He may lighten your load.

Jesus had time for both the important (Jairus) and the seemingly insignificant (the unnamed woman). Jesus has time for you. And he knows you. He is able to balance everyone's needs to provide for each person in the right way and at the right time.

Prayer: Jesus, I place my concerns into your hands. Answer me in the way you know is best for me. Amen.

A.J.D.

For further reading, see The People's Bible commentary on Mark, pages 75-81.

Jesus Turns Death Into Sleep

Bible Reading: Mark 5:21-43

He went in and said to them, "Why all this commotion and wailing? The child is not dead but asleep." (Mark 5:39)

41 He took her by the hand and said to her, *"Talitha koum!"* (which means "Little girl, I say to you, get up!"). 42 Immediately the girl stood up and began to walk around. (Mark 5:41-42)

She really was dead. The messengers who told Jairus, "Your daughter is dead" (5:35), surely knew the difference between dead and asleep. The people at the house who were crying and wailing loudly knew the difference. They had seen sleep before, and they had seen death before. This was death. They laughed when Jesus suggested otherwise. Yet Jesus still said it: "The child is not dead but asleep."

People usually see a big difference between sleep and death. Many fear death. Few fear sleep. Sleep is temporary. Death is final. That's how we usually think about it. By saying that the dead girl was asleep, Jesus was making a bold claim that he could make death temporary. He spoke and "immediately the girl stood up and began to walk around." That's all it took—Jesus' Word.

By the power of Jesus' Word, there is no difference between death and sleep. Because Jesus took away sin's punishment with his death on the cross, those connected to Jesus will wake up. Jesus once said, "I am the resurrection and the life. The one who believes in me will live, even though they die" (John 11:25).

If you are old enough to read this, you have already fallen asleep thousands of times. You know how it works. You close your eyes. You sleep. You wake up. Then you do it all again. Close your eyes. Sleep. Wake up. It has happened so many times that most people have no doubt that they will wake up. That's just what happens when you sleep. And that's just what will happen when you die. You can face the hour of your death the same way you face the hour you go to bed. You don't know exactly when you will fall asleep, but you know that you will wake up. When you die, Jesus will open your eyes and you will see the new eternal day of paradise. Jesus has promised it, and Jesus can do it. Don't be afraid! Jesus turns death into sleep.

Prayer: Jesus, make me ready for my last hour. Give me confidence that I too, because of your death and resurrection, will rise to live with you forever. Amen.

A.J.D.

For further reading, see The People's Bible commentary on Mark, pages 75-81.

How Well Do You Know Jesus?

Bible Reading: Mark 6:1-6

"Isn't this the carpenter? Isn't this Mary's son and the brother of James, Joseph, Judas and Simon? Aren't his sisters here with us?" And they took offense at him. (Mark 6:3)

Sometimes those who think they know Jesus the best do not know him well at all. This was the case in Nazareth, the town where Jesus grew up. The people in Nazareth had known Jesus his entire life. To them, he wasn't the authoritative teacher. He was Mary's son. He was the carpenter, the brother of Mary's other children, the kid they had seen grow up in their small town. They knew him well. At least, they thought they did. They weren't ready to accept his authority because it contradicted the picture of him they already had in their minds. So they took offense at him. And in doing so, they missed out on the wonderful blessings of his Word.

Sometimes those who think they know Jesus the best do not know him well at all. The temptation is lurking for you too! How well do you know Jesus? If you have known him your whole life, you probably know the Lord's Prayer and the Apostles' Creed by heart. But do you know it so well that you recite it without thinking? You may not fully understand the enormous concepts coming from your lips. Those who think they know it all already may hear God's law condemning a sin of which they are guilty, but then they think, "I know I'm forgiven, so it doesn't really matter what I do." Perhaps when you hear the words and works of Jesus, you immediately reduce your mental effort because, after all, you already know how the story goes. But then you are missing out on how breathtaking and surprising Jesus really is! Every time you hear his Word, you are different than the last time—a little older, with more experiences and interactions in your past. Listen! He is speaking to you! There is always more to learn about Jesus.

Keep up the mental effort as you listen, because Jesus said that it's through listening to his Word that he accomplishes all the promises and gifts that he offers. His teachings are for you, no matter how well you know Jesus. He doesn't say, "You know me already. I need to turn my attention to unbelievers." He says, "Here is my body and blood, given and shed *for you*." He says, "I forgive *your* sins." Hear it as if it's new. Jesus has wonderful things for you too. You can't know him too well.

Prayer: Holy Spirit, give me eager ears and a clear mind to gladly hear and learn the Word of Christ. Amen.

A.J.D.

For further reading, see The People's Bible commentary on Mark, pages 81-83.

Jesus Was Rejected Too

Bible Reading: Mark 6:1-6

He could not do any miracles there, except lay his hands on a few sick people and heal them. [6] He was amazed at their lack of faith. Then Jesus went around teaching from village to village. (Mark 6:5-6)

Even Jesus was rejected. In more than one place, the Scriptures say that Jesus was a good preacher. He preached with authority. He got people's attention. Yet sometimes Jesus was rejected. Sometimes it looked as if he was a failure. "He could not do any miracles" in Nazareth, except a few healings, because the people didn't have the faith to go to him for help. Jesus was rejected, but it wasn't because he made a mistake. It wasn't because he went about things the wrong way. Jesus simply and honestly spoke the truth, and he spoke it well. But the people in Nazareth rejected him.

Should we expect anything different? The Son of God was rejected, and the apostles were too. (Read the book of Acts to see how often!) Should we think that if we just get the right kind of pastor, package God's Word in the right way, and try to hide things that may be offensive, people will then follow and believe? Rejection is normal! Rejection doesn't mean that a mistake has been made in the preaching or teaching of the gospel. It has always been this way. Moses, Elijah, Jeremiah, Ezekiel, and many others in the Old Testament were rejected when they relayed the exact message God had told them to proclaim. Should we expect anything different? Sometimes Christians who present the simple, honest truth of God's Word will be rejected too.

But here's what our God is like: He can do amazing things with rejection. Rejection does not equal defeat for God. It does not mean failure. Rejection of God's Word and of God's people, when it comes, is just the next thing God will use for the good of his kingdom and his people. After Jesus was rejected in Nazareth, several other villages were able to hear his Word. Jesus' rejection ultimately led to his arrest, condemnation, and death. God had in mind to use the rejection for Jesus' good and for your good—for your salvation won on the cross.

If you face rejection for a simple and honest presentation of God's Word, you are not the first! You can trust that God can and will use the rejection for good. Stick with the simple and honest presentation! Don't be discouraged! Stand firm in the simple, honest truth of God's Word.

Prayer: Jesus, give me courage to stand firm in the truth of your Word, even when I face rejection for it. Amen.

A.J.D.

For further reading, see The People's Bible commentary on Mark, pages 81-83.

Trust Jesus' Commands

Bible Reading: Mark 6:7-13

Calling the Twelve to him, he began to send them out two by two and gave them authority over impure spirits. 8 These were his instructions: "Take nothing for the journey except a staff—no bread, no bag, no money in your belts." (Mark 6:7-8)

Picture your car as you leave for vacation. How many bags are loaded in the back? How many snacks are strategically positioned in the front? You have clothes, personal care items, phones, games, chargers, food, an emergency kit, and at least one credit card in case you think of something later. Days of planning, hours of packing, but when you start driving away from home, you still have the nagging feeling that you are forgetting something important, something you need for the trip to work out.

Jesus sent the twelve apostles on their first ministry trip; they each were to take a walking stick and the clothes they were wearing. That's it. No bags, no snacks, and not even money to buy provisions. It seems foolish, but Jesus told them to do it; therefore, it would work out. It's that simple. They had no supplies, but they had Jesus' command. If Jesus told them to do it, they could trust that it was the right thing to do and a good thing to do. So they went. They followed Jesus' command. They may not have known how it would work out, but by the end it did. People took care of them along the way, and their mission was successful.

By sending the apostles out with nothing this first time, Jesus was training them to rely on him for success in their later ministries. He would not always be with them in person, but they would always have his Word.

That Word, both the commands and the promises, can be trusted. Scripture does not tell you to follow only the commands of God that make sense to you or only the ones that are easy for you to follow—that would be fearing and trusting your perspective more than God's. You can trust all God's commands and promises. He does not leave you hopeless or alone when you follow his will. He promises to provide for you. He once said, "Seek first his kingdom and his righteousness, and all these things will be given to you as well" (Matthew 6:33). You do not need to disobey in order for things to work out. Obey his commands and he will provide. That's his promise.

Prayer: Lord God, help me trust your Word—both your commands and your promises—even when it is difficult. Amen.

A.J.D.

For further reading, see The People's Bible commentary on Mark, pages 83-88.

Does God Love Me?

Bible Reading: Mark 6:14-29

When the daughter of Herodias came in and danced, she pleased Herod and his dinner guests.

The king said to the girl, "Ask me for anything you want, and I'll give it to you." [23] **And he promised her with an oath, "Whatever you ask I will give you, up to half my kingdom."**

[24] **She went out and said to her mother, "What shall I ask for?"**

"The head of John the Baptist," she answered. (Mark 6:22-24)

Listen to what Jesus said about John the Baptist in Matthew 11:11: "Truly I tell you, among those born of women there has not risen anyone greater than John the Baptist." What a high honor! Jesus himself considered John to be great. If someone is so great in the eyes of Jesus, how would you expect that person to die? Perhaps a quiet, peaceful death. Or maybe the person would live up to that greatness by making a bold stand for Christ and dying as a martyr and an example for the church.

Look at how John died. He was in prison for being honest about an illicit relationship between King Herod and Herodias. Then he was executed, not because he proclaimed God's Word but because that insignificant ruler made a foolish, spontaneous oath when an exotic dancer pleased him. How random! How unfair!

From John's perspective, doesn't it seem that God must have forgotten about him? But remember Jesus' words: John was the greatest. Yet he languished in prison and died in such a cruel and random way. That tragedy was not a reflection of how Jesus felt about him.

In the same way, bad things that happen to you are not a reflection of how God feels about you. It may seem natural to track all the cruel and random things that happen in your life and declare, "God must not love me!" But that would be an incorrect conclusion. Bad things happen, even to good people—they are not a commentary on God's feelings toward you.

Then where do you find evidence of how God feels about you? Look at the cross. There God demonstrated his love for you. Christ died for you. God did not spare his own Son but gave him up for you. Look to the cross for evidence, and go to his Word for confirmation. His Word overrules your feelings and your sight. Remember your baptism, when God promised that he would remain your Father. Because of Jesus, nothing—neither life nor death, neither the present nor the future, not even Herod's godless oath—can separate you from the love of God.

Prayer: Lord, help me rely on your Word alone. Amen.

A.J.D.

For further reading, see The People's Bible commentary on Mark, pages 89-92.

Jesus Has Compassion

Bible Reading: Mark 6:30-34

When Jesus landed and saw a large crowd, he had compassion on them, because they were like sheep without a shepherd. So he began teaching them many things. (Mark 6:34)

Jesus and his apostles must have been exhausted. They had just returned from their mission trip. During that time, Jesus had been teaching and crowds had followed him wherever he went. Mark wrote, "So many people were coming and going that they did not even have a chance to eat" (6:31). It was time for them to get away by themselves. They hopped into a boat in search of a quiet place where they could be alone. As it turns out, a quiet and solitary place was hard to find. "Many who saw them leaving recognized them and ran on foot from all the towns and got there ahead of them" (6:33). They needed a break. They needed time alone. But the crowds followed.

"When Jesus landed and saw a large crowd . . ."—what would you have done if you were Jesus in this situation? How should this sentence end? "When Jesus landed and saw a large crowd" . . . he explained that he needed some time alone right now . . . he rolled his eyes and reluctantly talked with them . . . he got back in the boat and went the other way, pretending he didn't notice them . . . he shouted with righteous indignation, "Please leave us alone for a few hours!"

Instead, "When Jesus landed and saw a large crowd, he had compassion on them." How amazing! How wonderful! He had compassion on the people who were interrupting his vacation time. Why didn't he get mad? Here's why: "He had compassion on them, because they were like sheep without a shepherd." In that crowd, he saw not inconvenience but individual souls that needed rest just as his disciples needed rest. "So he began teaching them many things." He saw "sheep without a shepherd." If real sheep have no shepherd, they will unknowingly wander into danger. They need someone to lead them to quiet pastures where they can eat and rest. Souls without the Good Shepherd will wander into danger and die. So Jesus took the time to care—to be that Shepherd of souls.

This is how Jesus treats you. He is not annoyed by you, and he will not ignore you. Instead, he sees you and has compassion on you. He has compassion because he sees what you're going through. He sees your struggles. He knows what you need. And he's never too busy to provide it. You are never an inconvenience to your Savior.

Prayer: Jesus, how gracious you are to have compassion on me! Thank you. Amen.

A.J.D.

For further reading, see The People's Bible commentary on Mark, pages 93-96.

Jesus Provides for Soul and Body

Bible Reading: Mark 6:30-44

They were like sheep without a shepherd. So he began teaching them many things. (Mark 6:34)

41 **Taking the five loaves and the two fish and looking up to heaven, he gave thanks and broke the loaves. . . .** 42 **They all ate and were satisfied.** (Mark 6:41-42)

A crowd of thousands gathered in front of Jesus. He called them sheep without a shepherd and taught them many things. He knew what they needed. Their souls needed his teaching. Later in the day, the disciples recognized that the people had been without food. They brought this to Jesus' attention. Then Jesus fed them. He knew what they needed. Their bodies needed food.

Jesus cares for both soul and body. That's who you are—you are both soul and body. You are not one without the other. Jesus cares for you—the whole you. He does not neglect one part to focus only on the other. He provides for your soul. He provides for your body.

When someone says that the soul is important and the body is not, that person is minimizing the gift of the physical body. Your body is you. It is important! When Jesus returns on the Last Day, your actual body will be raised and glorified, and you will live in a physical paradise with Jesus forever. All the hurt and shame and anxiety will be gone, but it will be your body. Take care of it as the gift of God that it is.

On the other hand, when someone spends time attending to only physical things and does not feed the soul, that person also is neglecting a part of himself or herself. The soul is a creation of God, a gift from him. Your soul is you. It gives you life, and it is where you find peace and comfort and joy. A person will not be whole without a healthy soul. Feed it with the Word of God, the Bread of Life.

What a comfort to know that Jesus cares for you, the whole you! Your heavenly Father knows what you need for both body and soul (see Matthew 6:25-34). He wants to give you good things to take care of both (see Matthew 7:7-12). He wants nothing more than to have you, both body and soul, in his presence in heaven to experience the full physical and spiritual joys that he has in store for you.

Prayer: Heavenly Father, feed my body and my soul. Strengthen each so that I may serve and trust you more completely. Amen.

A.J.D.

For further reading, see The People's Bible commentary on Mark, pages 93-96.

Jesus Gives Courage

Bible Reading: Mark 6:45-56

Immediately Jesus made his disciples get into the boat and go on ahead of him to Bethsaida, while he dismissed the crowd.
46 After leaving them, he went up on a mountainside to pray.
47 Later that night, the boat was in the middle of the lake, and he was alone on land.
48 He saw the disciples straining at the oars, because the wind was against them. Shortly before dawn he went out to them, walking on the lake. (Mark 6:45-48)

They all saw him and were terrified.

Immediately he spoke to them and said, "Take courage! It is I. Don't be afraid." (Mark 6:50)

What if the disciples had disobeyed Jesus? He made them get into the boat after he fed the five thousand, but what if they had said no? If they had stayed there, it's likely that the crowd would have treated them well. The people wanted to make Jesus king; the disciples certainly would have benefited from that. But they obeyed Jesus and got into the boat. They did the right thing, and that's when things got bad. Obedience resulted in a terror-filled, sleepless night of struggle in the middle of a lake. Disobedience would have been much easier and much more comfortable.

Still today, sometimes doing the right thing leads to a real struggle, while doing the wrong thing leads to short-term comfort. It takes courage to obey when you don't want to. It takes courage to do the right thing when you're going to be uncomfortable because of it. Where does that courage come from?

The disciples may have thought they were alone as they struggled, but they weren't. Jesus was out of their sight, but they were not out of his. The Savior was praying for them on the shore, and even though it was night, he saw them. He knew about the struggle. And at just the right time, he went out to them, walking on the water, so he could be even closer to them. Before stopping the wind, Jesus announced that he was there: "Take courage! It is I." It wasn't the end of the struggle that would bring courage. It was the presence of Jesus during it.

Obedience will at times lead to difficult, uncomfortable situations. But you will not struggle alone. Jesus even walks on water to be with those who listen to his voice. "Take courage! It is I," he says. He is there in the encouragement and instruction of his Word, in the bread and wine of the Sacrament, and in the announcement of forgiveness. It's Jesus. He is with you. That is where the courageous obedience comes from.

Prayer: Jesus, give me courage to obey you in all things. Amen.

A.J.D.

For further reading, see The People's Bible commentary on Mark, pages 96-99.

He Will Heal You

Bible Reading: Mark 7:31-37

He looked up to heaven and with a deep sigh said to him, "*Ephphatha!*" (which means "Be opened!").
35 At this, the man's ears were opened, his tongue was loosened and he began to speak plainly. (Mark 7:34-35)

Jesus healed many people, but there were many other people he did not heal. Jesus healed many people, but many of God's people today still suffer through physical maladies. Some can barely hear, some have trouble seeing, some can no longer walk.

Jesus' miracles did not guarantee that his people would be free of problems in this life. Rather, his miracles served as evidence that he was the Messiah, the Son of God. Isaiah wrote in the Old Testament about what would happen because of Jesus: "Then will the eyes of the blind be opened and the ears of the deaf unstopped. Then will the lame leap like a deer, and the mute tongue shout for joy" (Isaiah 35:5-6). This happened during the life of Jesus for some. It will happen for all of us later.

How can we be sure of that? Look at the extent of Jesus' power. He spoke to a deaf man. He spoke to ears that couldn't hear—a man who shouldn't have been able to respond. But the powerful Word of God called into existence hearing where there had been none. You have experienced this kind of miracle too. The voice of God spoke in Scripture and in Baptism, and that powerful Word called into existence faith where there had been none. Your heart responded to his voice. The blind see. The deaf hear. The mute speak. You believe.

Jesus used his power to do the most important miracle: giving you faith. Now you are guaranteed to be part of the full realization of that Isaiah prophecy. Jesus opened the eyes of your faith. The day is coming when he will open the physical eyes of those who don't see very well now. Those who have trouble hearing now will hear everything on the Last Day. Those who struggle to walk now can look forward to the day when they will be able to leap in the new heavens and the new earth. Those who can't speak well will shout for joy with no inhibition. You can look forward to a day when you will have perfect health.

Prayer: Lord God, thank you for the gift of faith. Give me strength and patience to live with my physical struggles now. Give me joy in looking forward to the day when you will make me whole. Amen.

A.J.D.

For further reading, see The People's Bible commentary on Mark, pages 106-108.

Jesus Uses People to Provide

Bible Reading: Mark 8:1-10

He told the crowd to sit down on the ground. When he had taken the seven loaves and given thanks, he broke them and gave them to his disciples to distribute to the people, and they did so. [7] They had a few small fish as well; he gave thanks for them also and told the disciples to distribute them. [8] The people ate and were satisfied. Afterward the disciples picked up seven basketfuls of broken pieces that were left over. [9] About four thousand were present. (Mark 8:6-9)

Another miraculous feeding! Jesus used seven loaves of bread and a few fish to feed thousands of people. And each person didn't receive only a bite. Everyone ate enough to be satisfied. And there were leftovers. This was a great miracle.

On the front lines of this miracle were Jesus' disciples. Jesus could have miraculously dropped the food in front of the people. He could have simply taken away their hunger. Instead, after miraculously multiplying the food, he used a very ordinary way to get the food to the people: The disciples handed it out. Jesus gave his disciples the privilege of being his hands. He used the disciples to provide for others.

Jesus likes to use people to provide for others. He provides for your soul and body through other people. Thank God for those people! Jesus alone accomplishes the miracle of securing forgiveness and creating faith, but he uses parents, pastors, teachers, and friends to distribute those gifts to you. These people have taught you the Word of God, baptized you, given you the Lord's Supper, pointed out your sin, and assured you of God's forgiveness. Jesus accomplishes the miracle of crops growing and animals reproducing, but he uses parents, spouses, friends, bosses, farmers, and workers to play a role in bringing physical benefits to you. They are his hands. He uses them to provide for you.

Jesus takes care of your physical and spiritual needs. Now he wants to use you to provide for others. Since he is taking care of you, you are able to live not for yourself but for Christ (2 Corinthians 5:15). One way you do that is by acting as his hands for whoever is around you. Provide encouragement, speak the truth in love, pray for individuals, give of your time for someone, and use your gifts and abilities to benefit someone else. Jesus likes to use you to provide for people. What a noble privilege and purpose you have!

Prayer: Heavenly Father, thank you for the people in my life who distribute your gifts to me. Guide me daily to be your hands for others. Amen.

A.J.D.

For further reading, see The People's Bible commentary on Mark, pages 108-111.

Seek First His Kingdom

Bible Reading: Mark 8:14-21

The disciples had forgotten to bring bread, except for one loaf they had with them in the boat.
[15] "Be careful," Jesus warned them. "Watch out for the yeast of the Pharisees and that of Herod."
[16] They discussed this with one another and said, "It is because we have no bread."
[17] Aware of their discussion, Jesus asked them: "Why are you talking about having no bread? Do you still not see or understand?" (Mark 8:14-17)

Jesus warned the disciples to watch out for the yeast of the Pharisees and Herod. The disciples didn't understand. On their minds was the embarrassment of forgetting to bring enough food. They seemed to have forgotten already how Jesus could provide food in sudden and unexpected ways. He had recently fed thousands of people on two separate occasions. If the lack of bread was the problem, Jesus could take care of it! How quickly concerns about earthly things took over the disciples' thoughts!

Jesus wasn't talking about bread. The yeast of the Pharisees and that of Herod were their teachings, which were contrary to the truth proclaimed by the Old Testament and by Jesus. Those false teachings were like yeast, because a little bit makes a big difference. A small amount of yeast works through a whole batch of dough and makes the entire thing rise. A seemingly small or insignificant false teaching would threaten to undermine Scripture as the reliable source of truth that it is. Jesus was urging the disciples to make faithfulness to his Word their priority. It should be yours too.

If that is your priority, what about everything else? If I insist on confessing all of God's Word to be true, won't I be ridiculed and isolated? If I keep my words and actions in line with God's will, won't I lose friends and the respect of peers? If I spend time in prayer and devotion, won't I run out of time to get everything else done? How quickly concerns about earthly things take over our thoughts!

Jesus once said, "Seek first his kingdom and his righteousness, and all these things will be given to you as well" (Matthew 6:33). By "all these things," Jesus was referring to all the earthly concerns that cause people to worry. Make faithfulness to Jesus' Word your priority. He can and will provide for the rest. He has done it before, in miraculous ways when necessary, and he will do it again. Trust this promise.

Prayer: Triune God, keep me faithful to your Word. Help me and my church avoid any false teaching, and give me confidence that you will provide for me. Amen.

A.J.D.

For further reading, see The People's Bible commentary on Mark, pages 112-114.

Jesus Knows Why

Bible Reading: Mark 8:22-26

He took the blind man by the hand and led him outside the village. When he had spit on the man's eyes and put his hands on him, Jesus asked, "Do you see anything?"

[24] He looked up and said, "I see people; they look like trees walking around."

[25]Once more Jesus put his hands on the man's eyes. Then his eyes were opened, his sight was restored, and he saw everything clearly. (Mark 8:23-25)

What a strange miracle! After Jesus touched the blind man, the Savior asked the man if he could see anything. The man responded that the people walking around looked like trees. So Jesus put his hands on the man again, and only then could the man see everything clearly. It seems as if the first try didn't work!

Why did Jesus do this miracle in two parts? Was he running low on power? Did he make a mistake the first time? Jesus is the Son of God. He could have healed this man in any number of ways. He had the power to do so instantaneously. However, he chose to do it this way on this occasion. Why? Mark didn't explain why. But Jesus knew why, and that's what matters.

Don't you wish you knew why God allows certain things to happen to you? Why do others have easier lives? Why do some problems linger? Why does he seem to work more powerfully in the lives of other people? He doesn't tell us, so we can't know for sure. But Jesus knows, and that's what matters.

Trusting Jesus means trusting not only that he will do what is good for you but also that he will do it the right way and at the right time. But, oh, sometimes we get so impatient! Sometimes Jesus works in stages, as he did for this blind man. He may not solve a problem in your life all at once but slowly over time. It's not because he doesn't have the power to do it instantaneously. It's because he knows how best to work in your life with his Word and his power. He gives attention to you as a unique individual and shows the willingness to spend time on you.

Perhaps one day you will be able to look back and say, "Now I see what he was doing! He knew exactly what I needed!" However, you may never know why God dealt with you the way he did. But he knows, and he understands. That's what matters.

Prayer: Jesus, work in my life with your Word and your power in just the right way and at just the right time. Amen.

A.J.D.

For further reading, see The People's Bible commentary on Mark, pages 114-115.

The Job Description

Bible Reading: Mark 8:31–9:1

He then began to teach them that the Son of Man must suffer many things and be rejected by the elders, the chief priests and the teachers of the law, and that he must be killed and after three days rise again. 32 He
spoke plainly about this, and Peter took him aside and began to rebuke him.
33 But when Jesus turned and looked at his disciples, he rebuked Peter. "Get behind me, Satan!" he said. "You do not have in mind the concerns of God, but merely human concerns." (Mark 8:31-33)

When a business posts a job opening, it includes a job description. Before you apply, you should know what you would be doing, what would be expected of you, and what qualifications you should have. Perhaps this is a position you wouldn't want to accept!

After teaching and performing miracles—enough to fill seven and a half chapters in the gospel of Mark—Jesus asked the disciples, "Who do you say I am?" Peter answered, "You are the Messiah." This gave Jesus an opportunity to explain the job description of the Messiah. He must suffer, be rejected, be killed, and rise again. A wonderful little word in that job description is *must.* It had to happen that way. The suffering, rejection, death, and resurrection were necessary. God saw no other option.

But is that true? Weren't there other options? Couldn't Jesus have overcome the opposition and avoided the suffering? Couldn't Jesus have asserted his power and ruled as king? This is what Peter wanted Jesus to do. As the Son of God, certainly Jesus had the ability to do it that way, but what would have been the result of his avoiding the suffering and death? Your sins would still cling to you, and you would have to pay for them in hell. It would bring you no comfort to see Jesus ruling as King if you had to pay for your own sins!

This is why Jesus said that wonderful little word *must.* In his mind, leaving you alone to pay for your own sins was not an option even to consider. He said he *must* fulfill the job description of the Messiah. God considered it necessary, because his single-minded purpose was to save you from your sins.

Jesus knew the job description, and he accepted the position anyway! How greatly he must love you!

Prayer: Jesus, thank you for taking on the role of Messiah. Help me keep in mind the concerns of God ahead of human concerns. Amen.

A.J.D.

For further reading, see The People's Bible commentary on Mark, pages 119-124.

Say No to Yourself

Bible Reading: Mark 8:31–9:1

Then he called the crowd to him along with his disciples and said: "Whoever wants to be my disciple must deny themselves and take up their cross and follow me." (Mark 8:34)

If you listen carefully to what Jesus says, this is one of the most difficult verses of Scripture to hear. Jesus gives us the job description of a Christian: Following Jesus means saying no to yourself. This is extremely difficult.

In the Old Testament, God said that every inclination of the human heart is evil. That means the natural, authentic version of you is someone whose mind and desires naturally go against God's will. We naturally, on our own, without thinking, tend toward disobedience. Following Jesus means saying no to yourself. Being Jesus' disciple means going against what may very well come naturally to you. Following Jesus means not being true to yourself.

When you want something that is different from what God wants for you, say no to yourself, not to God. You can't excuse sin by saying, "That's just who I am" or "It just feels right" or "I can't help it." If it is against God's will, it's wrong. Every person has certain sins that come very naturally. For one it might be angry outbursts; for another it may be subtly tearing down others. It might be sexual sin or addiction or arrogance. If you try to justify yourself by saying, "I'm just being true to myself," Jesus might say, "Exactly. That's the problem. Following me means saying no to yourself." Being a disciple means putting Jesus' Word, his commands, and his will first.

Being Jesus' disciple is not easy, but it is worth it. Yes, taking up your cross means denying yourself, but Jesus also said, "Follow me." Follow him to his cross. See him do the most unnatural thing: He willingly suffered hell when it was not deserved. He did it for you. God put you first. That's why he lived a perfect life—so that it can be given to you. That's why he died—so that you can be set free from God's punishment. That's why he gave commandments—because following them is what's best for you. That's why he told you to deny yourself—because no one else in this world is telling you that, because no one else in this world truly loves you the way Jesus does. No one knows what is really best for you in the long run better than Jesus. Following Jesus is worth it!

Prayer: Jesus, help me deny myself, take up my cross, and follow you. Amen.

A.J.D.

For further reading, see The People's Bible commentary on Mark, pages 119-124.

Jesus Is Serious About Sin

Bible Reading: Mark 9:30-50

"If anyone causes one of these little ones—those who believe in me—to stumble, it would be better for them if a large millstone were hung around their neck and they were thrown into the sea. [43] If your hand causes you to stumble, cut it off. It is better for you to enter life maimed than with two hands to go into hell, where the fire never goes out." (Mark 9:42-43)

If you would think that committing a sin is not a big deal, look at how serious Jesus is about sin. He is serious because hell is real. Jesus does not hide this truth, and we should not minimize it either. It doesn't matter how people feel about it. Hell is real whether you like it or not. If you give people the impression that sin is not a big deal, or if you prevent people from hearing the gospel or trusting Jesus, you are causing them to stumble. This is a serious offense. Jesus said it would be better to die a terrible death than to be the cause of someone's eternal death. That eternal death in hell must be dreadful, because Jesus said cutting off parts of the body would be better than suffering in hell.

Jesus is serious about sin. You should be too. The problem is that cutting off body parts won't stop you from sinning. Even with no hands, you would still have a sinful heart and mind. Even with no eyes, you would still have sinful thoughts and desires. The total corruption of the sinful nature is a serious problem.

Jesus is serious about this problem, so serious that he suffered hell to save you from it. He went to extreme lengths to save you. He wouldn't have done it if hell didn't exist or was no big deal. Jesus is serious about sin and about saving you from its consequences! It is good news that Jesus is so serious about sin!

Let's be serious about it too. Do whatever it takes to avoid it. Cutting off body parts may not work, but you may need to cut yourself off from friends or from situations that lead you to sin or pull you away from Christ. Then, be serious about sin by making the gospel more important than anything else. Spend time with the gospel of forgiveness for yourself. Then make sure others know that there is nothing more important than what Jesus did for them.

Prayer: Jesus, thank you for being serious about sin. Keep me from causing others to stumble, and help me avoid situations that cause me to stumble. Amen.

A.J.D.

For further reading, see The People's Bible commentary on Mark, pages 132-137.

One Thing You Lack

Bible Reading: Mark 10:17-31

"One thing you lack," he said. "Go, sell everything you have and give to the poor, and you will have treasure in heaven. Then come, follow me."

[22] **At this the man's face fell. He went away sad, because he had great wealth.** (Mark 10:21-22)

He was a good man. But Jesus said that he was missing one thing, and that one thing was preventing the man from being saved. Jesus didn't tell the man what it was; instead, he showed him: "Go, sell everything you have and give to the poor, and you will have treasure in heaven." The man went away sad. He couldn't do what Jesus told him to do because he loved his wealth so much. The man could claim to keep a lot of the commandments. Honoring his parents, not stealing, giving of his time and energy to others—these were sacrifices he could make. These were easy because they didn't involve giving up what he treasured most. He still had his wealth. Jesus knew the man's heart, so Jesus told the man to give up the very things he treasured most. The man's reaction to this command revealed something important. When the man walked away from Jesus sad, he revealed that his heart was divided. Jesus proved what had first place in the man's heart. He didn't need to sell his stuff to earn heaven. He needed to love God above all things.

There are a lot of commandments you can keep and a lot of sacrifices you can make without much difficulty because they don't require you to give up what you love most. Money, family, reputation, intelligence, independence—what is it that you love most? If that treasure were threatened, your reaction would give you away too. One thing you lack, a very important thing: a heart completely undivided and devoted to God. No one has kept the First Commandment; then how can anyone enter eternal life?

You can because God has revealed something important. He has revealed his undivided heart. He doesn't just tell you about his love. He showed you. He gave up everything for you. He willingly gave up his divine power and became a human so he could be your substitute in life, keeping the First Commandment and giving you the credit for it. Then Jesus gave up even life itself so that he could be your substitute in death and receive your punishment for broken commandments.

All people lack the one thing necessary to enter eternal life, but God has provided it for you.

Prayer: God, my Savior, thank you for your undivided heart. Give me a heart that treasures you above all things. Amen.

A.J.D.

For further reading, see The People's Bible commentary on Mark, pages 142-145.

More Evidence of Jesus' Love

Bible Reading: Mark 10:17-31

Jesus looked at him and loved him. "One thing you lack," he said. (Mark 10:21)

The man thought he had kept the commandments; Jesus looked at him and loved him. Jesus loved the man so much that the Savior told him he was wrong. Jesus' love for the man refused to allow him to continue thinking he was okay. Jesus' love compelled him to point out the man's sin. By telling him to sell his possessions, Jesus showed the man that he loved his wealth more than he loved Jesus. And if he loved something more than God, he could not earn eternal life. Something needed to change.

Jesus' love is not just a feeling. Jesus' love is an action. It is doing what is best for a person. Jesus loved the man, so he did what was best for him. That's why Jesus said something that hurt. Jesus cared so much about the man that he told him the truth. He pointed out sin so the man could admit the sin, receive forgiveness, and then trust that forgiveness as the reason he would have eternal life rather than trusting in his own goodness.

Jesus points out sin because he loves you. He cares about you more than anyone else does. Others may think they are helping you by telling you that you can do and believe whatever you want, but that attitude leads to breaking God's commands and being separated from him for eternity. Jesus loves you enough to tell you the truth, even when it hurts, because he doesn't want to see you separated from him.

What can you do when a Christian you know and care about is caught in a sin? Love him or her. That means doing what is best for that person. The end goal of your words and actions is not to humiliate or tear down that person or make yourself look or feel better. The end goal is repentance and forgiveness, reconciliation with God, and a life of faithfulness to him. That's what is best. We should be clear that whatever sin it is, it is not okay. But you can be equally clear that you care, that you want to be by your neighbor's side to support. Support does not mean affirming the sin, but it means helping your neighbor fight against it and continuing to be a friend in every area of life.

Jesus looked at the rich young man and loved him. He loves you. Now love one another.

Prayer: Jesus, give me humility to listen to your loving rebuke and give me courage to love others as you love me. Amen.

A.J.D.

For further reading, see The People's Bible commentary on Mark, pages 142-145.

How to Be Great

Bible Reading: Mark 10:35-45

"Whoever wants to become great among you must be your servant, [44] and whoever wants to be first must be slave of all. [45] For even the Son of Man did not come to be served, but to serve, and to give his life as a ransom for many." (Mark 10:43-45)

The disciples James and John wanted to be great. To them, greatness meant having authority and being well known. They asked Jesus for the honor of sitting at his right and left in his glory. They wanted to be famous and powerful, able to walk through a crowd and have people look at them with respect and admiration. Their thoughts were on what they were going to get out of it. They thought greatness would benefit them.

Jesus' definition of greatness is different. According to Jesus, greatness is all about the other person. If you want to be truly great, you can't focus on yourself. "Whoever wants to become great among you must be your servant." If you are great, your focus will be on someone else.

Like the disciples, many of us would like to be known for being good at something, even for being great. When people see you, you want them to think, "I like her" or "I respect him." This is measuring greatness by what you receive from others. The focus is on you.

Jesus demonstrates greatness this way: "Even the Son of Man did not come to be served, but to serve." This is what the gospel of Mark is all about. Every miracle, every lesson, every sermon, every action was calculated to accomplish what someone else needed most. Jesus always had the cross as his goal. For him, the cross was not about his suffering. It was all about your salvation and your forgiveness. He did not come to be served, but to serve, and to be a ransom for many. For you.

That ransom frees you from having to prove that you're great. It frees you simply to be great. It frees you from needing to focus on what you are doing. It frees you to focus on what an individual family member or colleague needs. You are free to put each of them ahead of you, to be a servant of all, because Jesus has already put you first.

Be great during the next 24 hours. Other people may not notice (though several probably will). But Jesus does.

Prayer: Lord God, give me the humility to follow you, to serve others, and to be truly great. Amen.

A.J.D.

For further reading, see The People's Bible commentary on Mark, pages 146-149.

Triumphant and Willing

Bible Reading: Mark 11:1-11

Those who went ahead and those who followed shouted, "Hosanna!"

"Blessed is he who comes in the name of the Lord!"

10 "Blessed is the coming kingdom of our father David!"

"Hosanna in the highest heaven!" (Mark 11:9-10)

Jesus entered Jerusalem in the middle of a triumphant scene. People spread clothes and branches on the road in front of the colt he was riding as if Jesus were a king, a son of David. The crowds shouted cheers and quoted psalms that predicted the arrival of the Messiah. Sometimes this is referred to as the "triumphal entry." The parade seems to live up to that description.

But consider what was at the end of this entrance. Jesus was entering Jerusalem to die. We would hardly consider that triumphant! But it is triumphant for you because Jesus' death removed from you the liability for your sin. You get the victory of eternity in God's presence! That's triumph! And if it is triumph for us, then it is triumph for Jesus too, because his purpose was to reconcile you to God. He accomplished that! Jesus took up his throne, not by grabbing political power but by becoming the Savior of all through his suffering and death.

Jesus knew what would happen when he entered Jerusalem, but he entered anyway. The events of the week did not take him by surprise. Three times in Mark chapters 8-10 Jesus plainly and clearly told his disciples that he would be rejected, suffer, and die. As he entered Jerusalem, he knew what the people would do to him. He knew what was in their hearts. He knew the torment he would endure. Jesus had the chance to turn around and avoid Jerusalem, but he didn't. He entered willingly.

Jesus also knows that you have betrayed him and disobeyed him. He knows that you desire to do things that are contrary to his Word. He had the chance to avoid you too, but he didn't. He came to you through your baptism. And he will not turn away from you today. He still wants to enter your heart through the Word of God and the Sacrament of the Lord's Supper. He comes to you willingly, not to punish you but to give you the triumph of forgiveness.

Jesus entered Jerusalem triumphantly and willingly—and it was for you. He wants to enter your heart in the same way. Receive him gladly as you hear his Word and receive his Sacrament. He will not turn away from you!

Prayer: Jesus, come to me through your Word and sacrament, and give me joy from your presence. Amen.

A.J.D.

For further reading, see The People's Bible commentary on Mark, pages 151-155.

He Sent His Son

Bible Reading: Mark 11:27–12:12

"He had one left to send, a son, whom he loved. He sent him last of all, saying, 'They will respect my son.'
[7] "But the tenants said to one another, 'This is the heir. Come, let's kill him, and the inheritance will be ours.' [8] So they took him and killed him, and threw him out of the vineyard." (Mark 12:6-8)

A few days before his death, Jesus told this parable of the tenants. It's a sad, tragic story, but the actions of one character in particular defy explanation.

A man owned a vineyard and rented it out to tenant farmers while he was away. He sent servants to collect fruit from the vineyard. The tenants beat and mistreated the servants, one after another. Inexplicably, the owner kept sending servants. The tenants even killed one of them! So what did the owner do? He sent his son! How careless! How foolish! Shouldn't he have known better? We almost want to shout, "No! What are you thinking? Don't send your son! Don't you see what they will do to him?"

Jesus told this parable, but it might not seem very realistic. No owner would be that foolish, right? No one would send his son into such a situation, would he? That's the point. God is that owner, and he is unlike any other. What we see in this parable is God's patience and God's determination to save. In the Old Testament, God repeatedly sent prophets to warn the people of their sin and call them to repentance. Time after time, the people refused to listen. They even mistreated the prophets God had sent. Instead of giving up on the people, God the Father sent his Son, knowing full well the suffering he would endure. He was determined to declare all people not guilty of sin, no matter the cost. And so he sent his Son.

Marvel at the patience and determination of the Father! Now think about what that means for you. What kind of treatment do you deserve from him? You also are guilty of repeated sins. You too have ignored the Word and commands of God when it pleased your sinful nature. What should God do with you?

The Father does what might sound foolish, but it is wonderful for you and me. He is patient with you, just as he was patient in the parable. He sent his Son for those who rejected him. He sent his Son for you.

Prayer: Heavenly Father, thank you for sending your Son. Help me receive your Word and commands with joy and obedience. Amen.

A.J.D.

For further reading, see The People's Bible commentary on Mark, pages 161-166.

Both God and Government

Bible Reading: Mark 12:13-17

Then Jesus said to them, "Give back to Caesar what is Caesar's and to God what is God's." (Mark 12:17)

At the time of Jesus, Israel was part of the Roman Empire. Rome was the authority. Many Jews in Israel despised Rome as a godless tyrant over God's people. Others were in favor of Roman rule. The two sides joined together to trap Jesus when some Pharisees and Herodians asked Jesus if it was right to pay taxes to the Roman government. If Jesus would have said they should pay taxes, he would have upset many Jews who thought they owed allegiance only to God. If Jesus would have said they should not pay taxes, they may have been able to charge him before the authorities. Either way, Jesus would have been discredited before one group or the other.

Jesus recognized the trap and gave a perfect answer, the correct answer. It was not an either-or answer, but a both-and answer. "Give back to Caesar what is Caesar's and to God what is God's." Since God instituted the authority of government, obeying the government is obeying God. (See Romans 13:1-7.)

Jesus' statement was not a political one, but a theological one. Yes, they should give to Caesar, even though their taxes went to a government that viewed the emperor as a god and that enacted policies that oppressed believers in the true God. Each one of us owes obedience to our leaders even when laws are made by corrupt, immoral, and godless leaders. You owe respect and honor even when you disagree with the policies of the leader, the lifestyle of the leader, or the way the leader came into power. Christians certainly may try to bring new leaders into office through honest and legal means, but while anyone is in power, you obey God by obeying the government.

At the same time, give to God. Give to God your trust that his commands are good and right and that when we obey authorities, it will be for the greater good. Give to God your sin, because he forgives even your disobedience and disrespect. Give to God your whole self so that you are guided by his Word and not by your emotions or opinions. Give to God your prayers, that he would provide for us honest and godly leaders in our homes, our churches, and our government.

We owe obedience and honor to both God and government. God grant us the ability to do it!

Prayer: Lord God, work in me a God-pleasing attitude toward my leaders. Give my leaders wisdom and boldness to do what is right and good. Amen.

A.J.D.

For further reading, see The People's Bible commentary on Mark, pages 166-169.

The God of the Living

Bible Reading: Mark 12:18-27

Jesus replied, "Are you not in error because you do not know the Scriptures or the power of God?" (Mark 12:24)

26 **"Now about the dead rising—have you not read in the Book of Moses, in the account of the burning bush, how God said to him, 'I am the God of Abraham, the God of Isaac, and the God of Jacob'?**
27 **He is not the God of the dead, but of the living."** (Mark 12:26-27)

The Sadducees who approached Jesus did not believe in the resurrection of the dead. They had the opinion that when you die, you're dead. They were certain that the dead body decays and stays right where it ends up after the funeral. People today often have the same view of death: It's the end. This is why so many people spend so much time, money, and worry trying to avoid death, or at least to postpone it as long as possible. They consider death to be the end of life, the end of joy, the end of experiences. To soften the blow of death, people may say that the deceased person's spirit is still with us, but underneath that statement is the opinion that we will never see the actual person anymore.

Jesus tells us something different. Death is not the end. There is a resurrection. We even say in the Apostles' Creed, "I believe in . . . the resurrection of the body." We know the Scriptures and the power of God. He has raised people from the dead before; he certainly can do it again! Both the Old and New Testaments teach that the physical bodies of people will come alive again on the Last Day.

Jesus pointed to one such place in the Old Testament. Abraham, Isaac, and Jacob had died more than four hundred years before God spoke to Moses, yet God could still say, "I am their God." If he still is their God, then their existence must not be over. Jesus used this to prove that the dead will rise.

When someone you love dies in the Lord, you have more than memories to hold on to. You have a resurrection to look forward to. The body will come back to life. The Bible says it! God has the power to make it happen! When you die, it will not be the end. In fact, you have more than a spiritual heaven to look forward to. Your physical body will rise to live with all the faithful before God in righteousness and purity forever.

Prayer: Lord, keep me faithful until death, that I may rise to be with you forever. Amen.

A.J.D.

For further reading, see The People's Bible commentary on Mark, pages 169-172.

The Greatest Commandments

Bible Reading: Mark 12:28-34

"To love him with all your heart, with all your understanding and with all your strength, and to love your neighbor as yourself is more important than all burnt offerings and sacrifices."

34 When Jesus saw that he had answered wisely, he said to him, "You are not far from the kingdom of God." (Mark 12:33-34)

Ask a mother who her favorite child is, and you will probably get a response similar to this: "Each and every one of my children is special to me." Ask Jesus what the greatest commandment is and you might expect a similar response: "They are all important!" After all, they are God's commandments. Aren't all of God's words important?

A teacher of the law did ask Jesus what the most important commandment was. Jesus didn't answer as we might expect. He actually picked out not just one commandment, but the top two! "Love the Lord your God with all your heart and with all your soul and with all your mind and with all your strength" and "Love your neighbor as yourself" (12:30-31). These are the greatest because they summarize everything God wants us to do. Every commandment is either a "love God above all things" commandment, a "love your neighbor as yourself" commandment, or a mixture of the two.

This means that keeping God's commandments requires you to do only two things: love God and love others. However, these may be the toughest two things to do. Your sinful nature doesn't want God to be the guide for your life. Your sinful nature wants you to serve yourself. It wants you to do whatever you want to do. It does not want to live by anyone else's standard of right and wrong. Knowing the two greatest commandments does not mean you can keep them.

That's why Jesus told the teacher of the law that he was not far from the kingdom of God—he was close, but not quite there yet. The man knew the two greatest commandments, but he couldn't keep them. No one can, except for Jesus. He brings you into his kingdom by giving you his perfect record of commandment-keeping and his punishment on the cross for your imperfect record. Because Jesus was your substitute, God now sees you as having kept the two greatest commandments with no sin left to punish.

So now that you have been cleansed from sin and brought into God's kingdom, you can use the two greatest commandments as an easy-to-remember guide and goal: Love God and love your neighbor. Let these two commandments guide your words and actions as you live in God's kingdom.

Prayer: Jesus, give me the opportunities and the ability to love you and my neighbor today. Amen.

A.J.D.

For further reading, see The People's Bible commentary on Mark, pages 172-174.

David's Son and David's Lord

Bible Reading: Mark 12:35-37

"Why do the teachers of the law say that the Messiah is the son of David? [37] David himself calls him 'Lord.' How then can he be his son?" (Mark 12:35,37)

It sounds like a riddle. Can you answer it? The Messiah is called the Son of David, but David called the Messiah his Lord. If the Messiah is a descendant of David, why would David call him Lord? Which is more accurate—is he David's Son or David's Lord?

Jesus is the Messiah, and this riddle tells us something about him. He was rightfully called the Son of David because God had given David a specific promise that one of his descendants would be the Messiah. Jesus was born into David's family tree. At the same time, Jesus is rightfully called David's Lord because he is not just a human being. He is also the true God who took on flesh. Therefore, he is still David's Lord. This riddle teaches that Jesus is both David's Son and David's Lord because he is 100 percent true man and 100 percent true God.

This riddle also tells us something about David. He was certainly a great king and a hero to the Israelites, but he needed a Lord too. He needed someone to be his Savior and King. Even though he was a great king, he occasionally let other things rule over him. He allowed his pride to rule him when he made a show of counting his army. He allowed his lust to rule him when he saw his neighbor Bathsheba from his rooftop. He allowed his arrogance to rule him when he believed he could cover up his sin. David knew he needed a King and a Savior. And so he called his Son "Lord" because he knew and trusted that the Messiah would wash away all his iniquity and cleanse him from his sin.

You too have let other things rule over you. If we could print out a record of your thoughts, what would dominate them? What fills your calendar? What motivates your purchases? These can reveal your lord. Materialism, greed, peer pressure, and achievement all demand your time, energy, and money. Too often we serve those demands.

For that reason, Jesus became your Lord. He planned out and executed your salvation completely, taking care of every consideration. He needed to live under the law and take credit for your sin, so he became human. He needed to be sinless to be the perfect substitute, and he was sinless because he is true God. He is David's Son and David's Lord. Jesus Christ, true God and true man, is your Lord.

Prayer: Lord God, thank you for planning out my salvation. Amen.

A.J.D.

For further reading, see The People's Bible commentary on Mark, pages 174-177.

The Widow's Offering

Bible Reading: Mark 12:41-44

Calling his disciples to him, Jesus said, "Truly I tell you, this poor widow has put more into the treasury than all the others." (Mark 12:43)

In school, children learn how to draw greater than (>) and less than (<) symbols to compare amounts: 5 > 2 and 8 < 12. It's simple math.

Jesus was watching people give their offerings, and he made a comparison. He saw rich people give large amounts of money. He saw a widow put in a few cents. This seems like an easy math problem. But Jesus made an apparently absurd statement. He said the widow put in more than the rich people. He explained it this way: "They all gave out of their wealth; but she, out of her poverty, put in everything—all she had to live on" (12:44).

Jesus was watching people give offerings, and he cares about what you do with your money. He even cares about the amount that you give as an offering, but the amount is not the bottom line. He sees what the amount says about your heart.

There is a warning here for you. Giving a lot of what you have does not mean that Jesus thinks you give a lot. You might give more than others, but if you already have more time or more talents or more wealth than others, you should be giving more than they are. The world might look at the bottom line, but Jesus sees the heart. He knows if your giving is too easy. If you still have a lot after the giving, perhaps it was no sacrifice at all. What does that say about your heart?

There is also a comforting promise here for you, especially if you have little to give—not much time, limited talents, or little wealth. When you make a sacrifice and offer even a little to the Lord, Jesus sees it as a lot. Maybe your offering at church isn't enough to pay someone's salary. Maybe the time you are able to give won't win you any service awards. Maybe the people around you seem more talented than you are. But Jesus does not need your offerings or your volunteer hours to change the world. He wants you, your heart. You show that he has it by making a sacrifice. It doesn't matter how much your giving accomplishes in the eyes of others. What matters is you are showing that God is worth the sacrifice, however large the bottom line is.

Prayer: Heavenly Father, help me trust that you will provide for me so that I may freely give of my time, my talent, and my treasure. Amen.

A.J.D.

For further reading, see The People's Bible commentary on Mark, pages 177-180.

She Did What She Could

Bible Reading: Mark 14:3-9

"She has done a beautiful thing to me. [8] She did what she could. She poured perfume on my body beforehand to prepare for my burial." (Mark 14:6,8)

Wouldn't it be wonderful if Jesus said about you what he said about this woman? "She has done a beautiful thing to me." Do you have what it takes to receive such recognition from the Son of God? Or are you not rich enough, talented enough, available enough, or important enough to do anything of value for Jesus?

Jesus said, "She did what she could." He praised her not for doing something impossible but for taking the opportunity that was right in front of her. She may not have had the means to travel great distances to preach. She may not have had the time to organize a food drive. She may not have had the ability to create an ad campaign for Jesus. But she did have perfume, so she used it.

She did what she could, not what others could. She did it willingly because she had been listening to Jesus. She believed his predictions that he was about to do what he could. As true God and true man, Jesus could be the Savior of all. He too took the opportunity that was right in front of him. Within days after this dinner, Jesus would be on the cross, bringing forgiveness and salvation to the world—to this woman, to you, to all. She had been listening to Jesus talk about his death, so she did what she could. She poured perfume on his body beforehand to prepare him for burial.

Jesus did what he could. He rescued you from hell. Now you can do what you can. There is no command that you go above and beyond your means and abilities. Jesus does not expect you to save the world. He did that. What are the opportunities in front of you? What do you have? Do you have money to give for the work of the church and to share with the less fortunate? Do you have the ability to fix something for the church or for a neighbor? Maybe what you can do is fight even harder against ever-present temptation. Do you have the opportunity to encourage someone to enter the ministry or to study for the ministry yourself? Can you welcome visitors at church?

Listen to the Word of God, believe what Scripture says, and then do what you can in service to God and to your neighbor.

Prayer: Jesus, open my eyes to opportunities to serve you and my neighbor. Amen.

A.J.D.

For further reading, see The People's Bible commentary on Mark, pages 193-196.

The Only Answer That Matters

Bible Reading: Mark 14:53-65

Jesus remained silent and gave no answer.

Again the high priest asked him, "Are you the Messiah, the Son of the Blessed One?"

62 "I am," said Jesus. "And you will see the Son of Man sitting at the right hand of the Mighty One and coming on the clouds of heaven."

63 The high priest tore his clothes. "Why do we need any more witnesses?" he asked. 64 "You have heard the blasphemy. What do you think?"

They all condemned him as worthy of death. (Mark 14:61-64)

When charged with a crime in a United States courtroom, people have the right to speak up in their own defense. They can also "plead the Fifth." This means that they are taking advantage of a clause in the Fifth Amendment that gives people the right to remain silent if an answer might incriminate them.

Jesus seems to have gotten this backward. When facing false accusations, Jesus remained silent. He didn't speak up in his own defense. But when faced with a question that could lead to a charge of blasphemy, Jesus did answer. "Are you the Messiah, the Son of the Blessed One?" Jesus answered with a powerful statement reminiscent of the great name the Lord gave to himself in the Old Testament: "I am." Jesus was claiming to be God. He spoke the truth—but the only answer he gave provided the high priest a reason to condemn Jesus to death. Why didn't Jesus say something before? Why didn't he remain silent now? Why did he answer this question and not the others? He passed on the opportunity to defend himself. He gave the priests a reason to condemn him!

That's exactly why! He wanted to go to the cross. He wanted to go there for you! Jesus was in complete control. He was going willingly to his death because that was the reason he was born. He wasn't on earth for his own personal comfort. He was there for you, just as he is always there for you. The only answer he gave is the only answer that matters. Jesus is God, and he wanted to die for you and for your salvation. He wanted to restore you to a good relationship with him though you could not earn it. Jesus wanted you to be able to look forward to the day he mentioned in the rest of his answer: "You will see the Son of Man sitting at the right hand of the Mighty One and coming on the clouds of heaven." That will not be a day of silence but of joyful celebration!

Prayer: Jesus, thank you for your willingness to suffer and die. Help me not remain silent about it. Amen.

A.J.D.

For further reading, see The People's Bible commentary on Mark, pages 209-213.

The Power of Sin

Bible Reading: Mark 14:66-72

He began to call down curses, and he swore to them, "I don't know this man you're talking about."
72 Immediately the rooster crowed the second time. Then Peter remembered the word Jesus had spoken to him: "Before the rooster crows twice you will disown me three times." And he broke down and wept. (Mark 14:71-72)

Everyone is born with original sin. This means that unless God works on us from the outside with his Word, we do not naturally trust him. Instead, we have a natural inclination to sin—to obey self rather than obey God. How strong is this inclination? Peter demonstrated its power in the high priest's courtyard while Jesus was on trial.

Peter denied that he knew Jesus. Only hours earlier, Jesus had told Peter that he would deny Jesus three times that night. Even after the warning, Peter still did it three times. It's even worse than that. After Jesus predicted Peter's denial, Peter had insisted emphatically that he would never do it. He went so far as to say he would die for Jesus before denying him, even if he was the only person left standing at Jesus' side. But only hours later he was calling down curses and swearing that he didn't know Jesus. When he remembered Jesus' words, Peter broke down and wept. What shame—what horror—when he realized how completely his sinful nature had controlled him!

The inclination of the sinful nature is strong. It's the inclination to serve self over serving God. You may wake up intending to be patient, but within an hour you find yourself yelling at your kids for their complaining. You may promise to avoid a certain sin, but the powers of the sinful nature and of habit diminish your will to fight the temptation. What shame!

Peter's story has a happy ending. Yours does too. After Jesus died and rose from the dead, he welcomed Peter back as a disciple, an apostle, and a child of God. Jesus welcomed Peter back after he died and rose precisely because he died and rose. Jesus died not only for Peter's denial but also for Peter's inclination to sin. Jesus' death has paid for your actual sins and your original sin. He has covered what you have done and who you are. His resurrection has given you a new life now and the guarantee of eternal life. His Word has worked on you from the outside, granting you forgiveness for all sin and providing you strength to fight against your natural inclination. Continue to fight! Then continue to trust Jesus for forgiveness.

Prayer: Lord God, help me fight against my sinful nature today. Give me a new heart that wants to serve you alone. Amen.

A.J.D.

For further reading, see The People's Bible commentary on Mark, pages 213-216.

Focus on the Cross

Bible Reading: Mark 15:1-32

And they crucified him. (Mark 15:24)

This is the pivotal moment in the history of humankind. It is the moment God already had in mind when he promised that someone would crush the serpent's head. It is the moment that changes everything for you. They crucified Jesus. Beaten, mocked, a crown of thorns pressed into his head, nails driven through his hands and feet—Jesus hung on a wooden cross until his body could no longer live.

Focus on the cross. What do you see there? First, see that sin is serious. It must be. Look at what it caused. The torments that Jesus suffered were the penalty for sin. When God deals with sin justly and fairly, it is a terrible thing! The Son of God suffered such great torments because of your sin. Your words, your behavior, your self-centeredness put Jesus on the cross. It is a terrifying thought! This is what you deserved.

Now look at the cross again. What do you see there? It's Jesus. Not you. Sin is being punished forever. It is getting what it deserves. And you are not there! What joy! What relief! Jesus willingly went to the cross so you would not have to suffer this. He took on your sin and served as your substitute when justice was served. What wondrous love is this! If sin was punished on this cross, then your sin must be gone. There is no punishment left. You will not get what you deserve. Jesus has won for you God's favor! What a joyful sight this cross is!

Look at the cross one more time. Now you can use it to provide strength and endurance in this life until you enter paradise. If your Savior was willing to suffer all this for you, you can suffer for a little while through temptation, rejection, pain, sickness, and trouble. He did more for you, and you can look forward to eternal glory because of it.

The cross is the pivotal moment in the history of humankind. It wipes clean your past, changes your present, and guarantees your future. Focus on the cross, and see that it is for you. Rejoice in the cross whenever you see its sign. Receive the Lord's Supper in remembrance of the cross, and hear the wonderful, personal words "given and poured out *for you*."

Prayer: Jesus, my Savior, hold your cross always before my eyes. Give me a proper attitude toward sin, joy in the forgiveness you freely give me, and endurance through the troubles I must bear. Amen.

A.J.D.

For further reading, see The People's Bible commentary on Mark, pages 216-225.

Jesus Is the Son of God

Bible Reading: Mark 15:33-39

When the centurion, who stood there in front of Jesus, saw how he died, he said, "Surely this man was the Son of God!" (Mark 15:39)

Mark began his gospel with these words: "The beginning of the good news about Jesus the Messiah, the Son of God" (Mark 1:1). One of Mark's purposes in writing was to prove that Jesus really is the Son of God. Jesus was not just a good human being. He was not just someone who had the Spirit of God in him. He was, in fact, God himself.

From the very beginning, Mark presented evidence for this truth. On two occasions, the voice of God from heaven identified Jesus as his Son. Evil spirits fell down before Jesus in terror because they knew who he was, and Jesus showed they were right in their assessments by driving them out of people. Jesus healed with a simple touch or a simple word. He taught with authority, and he claimed to have the authority to forgive sins. Jesus did not correct Peter when Peter called him the Messiah. Jesus gave perfect answers to smart people who were trying to trap him with challenging questions. When the high priest asked him if he was the Son of the Blessed One, Jesus answered with a blunt and powerful "I am." When he died, the curtain of the temple, separating humankind from God's presence, was torn in two from top to bottom. Yes, Mark proved his point with the evidence, and the centurion at the cross recognized it: "Surely this man was the Son of God!"

Who do you say Jesus is? Why does it matter? If Jesus truly is the Son of God, he has authority to distinguish between right and wrong. He has the authority to tell you how to live. Jesus is not simply a great man whose advice or suggestions you are free to follow or ignore. He is God. Ignoring or disobeying him has consequences.

Who do you say Jesus is? Why does it matter? If Jesus were only a man, even a great man, his death on the cross would do nothing for the problem of your sin. However, the centurion was right. Jesus is the Son of God. He was able to live a perfect life and credit that righteousness to your account. He was able to take on your sin and redeem you with his holy, precious blood and his innocent suffering and death. Jesus is the Son of God. That is good news for you!

Prayer: Jesus, Son of God, thank you for the gift of Mark's gospel. Increase my faith in the good news you have given through him. Amen.

A.J.D.

For further reading, see The People's Bible commentary on Mark, pages 225-228.

He Has Risen!

Bible Reading: Mark 16:1-8

"You are looking for Jesus the Nazarene, who was crucified. He has risen! He is not here. See the place where they laid him." (Mark 16:6)

"He has risen!" Is there a more triumphant phrase than this? Christians sing and shout it on Easter Sunday, often with tears in their eyes or chills down their spines. Let's not limit ourselves to basking in this statement only on Easter Sunday. There is no better news than the empty tomb. "He has risen" is not merely a statement about Jesus. It has something to say about you too.

"He has risen" says something about your sin. When Jesus died, your sin was on him. When Jesus rose, he did so with no sin on him. He is alive! He is no longer suffering, which means the sin is gone! The payment worked! Jesus is alive and your sin is buried. Sin has been conquered!

"He has risen" says something about your mortality. Jesus died, but then he physically came back to life. He has power over death. His resurrection guarantees that you too will rise, not just spiritually but physically. Your body will come back to life on the Last Day. It will be your body, but as with Jesus' glorified body, it will have no sin-stains left on it. You will live a physical eternity with Jesus! Death has been swallowed up in victory!

"He has risen" says something about your conscience. When Satan tries to accuse you of being not good enough, when your past tries to haunt you, you can point to the cross and the empty tomb. Yes, you have sinned, but Jesus has died and has risen! His Word, detailing the facts of his death and resurrection, answers Satan's accusations and overrules your feelings of inadequacy before God. He has declared you holy! The devil's work has been destroyed!

He has risen! Proclaim it on Easter with great joy and celebration. Proclaim it every Sunday because it is the reason we gather on the first day of the week. Proclaim it at funerals because it is the reason you again will see your loved ones who have died in the Lord. Rejoice in it every day because you have been baptized into his death and resurrection. "He has risen" gives you the victory, and it gives you the power to live a new life today.

Prayer: Triune God, thank you for the victory you have already given me through the resurrection of Jesus. Help me live a new life as your child today through the power of that resurrection. Amen.

A.J.D.

For further reading, see The People's Bible commentary on Mark, pages 230-236.

Seated at the Right Hand of God

Bible Reading: Mark 16:9-20

After the Lord Jesus had spoken to them, he was taken up into heaven and he sat at the right hand of God. (Mark 16:19)

Forty days after Jesus rose from the dead, he was taken up into heaven. For this reason, 40 days after Easter, the Christian church celebrates Ascension Day. This special day does not receive the same attention that is given to Christmas or Easter. It's not difficult to see why that is the case. It may seem like a strange thing to celebrate. Christmas and Easter are natural times to celebrate. Christ is born! Christ is risen! But what about Ascension? Christ is . . . gone?

No, Jesus' ascension does not mean that Jesus is gone. When he was taken up into heaven, he was seated at the right hand of God. The right hand of God is not a physical location. It is a place of honor, the position of all power and authority. While he was on earth, Jesus took on the form of a servant. Now that he is ascended and at the right hand of God, he has taken up all his divine power and authority. This means that although he is not visible, he is still with us. Instead of being contained by and located at one place, he now is present everywhere as true man and true God.

No longer a lowly servant, Jesus now uses the same power and authority that destroyed Pharaoh's army for the benefit of his people, his church. In his position of power and authority, he prays to God the Father for you, arranging everything to work for your good so that Satan and hell will not overcome you. No longer a servant confined to one place on earth, he gives his real body and blood to you every time you come to the Lord's Supper. Now ascended, he is working for you everywhere with unrivaled power. Ascension Day is a day for rejoicing!

After Jesus ascended into heaven, the disciples went out and preached. The last verse of Mark says that the Lord worked with them. He had ascended, yet he worked with them. We have confidence that the same is true today. When we preach, teach, and baptize, we are doing so with Christ's power and authority, and he is working with us. Let's make sure that our work continues until we see the risen and ascended Lord Jesus return.

Prayer: Lord Jesus, rule over all things for the benefit of your people on earth. Keep me faithful until the day you return in glory. Amen.

A.J.D.

For further reading, see The People's Bible commentary on Mark, pages 236-241.

People's
Bible
Devotions

Look for these other titles in the People's Bible Devotions series:

Old Testament
From the Beginning: God's Salvation Plan
Being the People of the Promise
Faithful God, Flawed Followers
Wisdom and Folly
Hope in Dark Times
God Has a Word for You

New Testament
He Is the Christ
The Gospel Knows No Boundaries
I Want to Know Christ
Until Christ Comes: Passing on the Gospel
You Are God's Special Possession
We Have Seen His Glory

Scan to view the series